Deadly Women
Volume Seven

20 Shocking
True Murder Cases

Robert Keller

Please Leave Your Review of This Book At
http://bit.ly/kellerbooks

ISBN- 9781089866213

© 2019 by Robert Keller

robertkellerauthor.com

Table of Contents

Sharee Miller

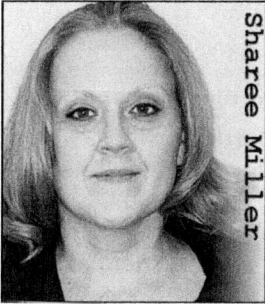

It has all the elements of a Hollywood movie and, indeed, it was made into one, albeit of the low-budget, made-for-TV variety. At its center, as in so many thrillers of this ilk, was a manipulative femme fatale, pulling the strings and making the men in her life dance like puppets. But Sharee Miller was no Kathleen Turner in Body Heat, no Sharon Stone in Basic Instinct. She was a dumpy, plain-looking mother-of-three, each of her kids sired by different fathers. How she was able to exert such control is difficult to fathom.

Sharee Miller was born in Michigan on October 13, 1971. She grew to be a precocious teen who left home at age sixteen and was married and the mother of a child by nineteen. That union, however, was never going to last. Not with Sharee's wild side and overtly flirty nature. Eventually, it broke down, and Sharee hit out on her own. Over the next few years, she'd bounce from one relationship to another, most of them of short duration. She'd also become pregnant twice and bear two children by different lovers. One of those men she married, but the marriage ended in divorce after her husband was convicted of child abuse. He had struck one of the children so hard that the child had suffered skull fractures.

By 1997, Sharee was 26 years old and the twice-divorced mother of three children. What she really needed in her life was some stability, someone to care for her and her kids, someone with money. That person arrived in the form of Bruce Miller, a successful businessman who owned B & D Salvage, an auto scrapyard in Flint, Michigan. Sharee started working there in late 1997. It wasn't long before she had her hooks in her new boss. Within a little over a year, she had accepted his proposal of marriage.

Bruce Miller was, by all accounts, a good man. He was absolutely besotted with his wife, who was 20 years his junior. For her part, Sharee was happy to have someone to cater to her needs. Not that it affected her behavior in any way. She remained a shameless flirt, fluttering her eyes at any man she encountered. She had also, by now, discovered the world of internet chat rooms and would spend hours online chatting with various men. That was how she met Jerry Cassaday.

Jerry was a former police officer from Cass County, Missouri. Once, he'd harbored aspirations of becoming an FBI agent, but those dreams had been dashed after he had broken a cardinal rule. He'd spoken out about wrongdoing and corruption within his department. For this gallant action, he was shunned, demoted, and eventually forced to resign. Depressed at losing the career he loved, he'd begun drinking heavily and even dabbling in drugs. That had ended up costing him his marriage. Thereafter, Cassaday had decided to make a fresh start and had moved to Reno, Nevada. He was working as a pit boss at Harrah's

Casino and Hotel when he first started communicating with Sharee Miller.

Like Sharee's husband, Jerry Cassaday was considered by those who knew him to be a nice guy. But he was lonely and vulnerable and thus easy pickings for the arch-manipulator. She told him that she was a wealthy businesswoman who was in a nonsexual marriage with an older, disabled man. She also peppered him with X-rated messages and videos, further drawing him into her web. When she started suggesting that they should meet in person, Jerry was all too keen.

An opportunity eventually presented itself when Sharee was invited to attend a Mary Kay convention in Reno. She had recently become an agent for the cosmetics company, and the junket was the perfect cover for an illicit hook-up. She and Jerry finally met face to face and had sex that first night. That was when Jerry learned that his internet buddy was every bit as kinky as her online persona had suggested.

In truth, Jerry Cassaday should have known better. He was an ex-cop and had once worked as a homicide investigator. He should have seen right through Sharee Miller, but Jerry was blinded by lust, blinkered by love. As he and Sharee resumed their online relationship (and managed a few more in-person visits), she began spinning him a tale. She told him that her husband was involved in the mob and that he was physically abusive to her. She used makeup to simulate bruises on her body and sent photos of these "injuries" to Jerry. She told him that she was pregnant with his child and sent him a fake sonogram (Miller was actually unable to have any more children because she'd had a tubal ligation). Then, just as Cassaday was getting excited about the child and urging her to leave her husband to be with him, she told him that her husband had paid some men to gang rape her and that she'd lost the baby as a result. She even set up a fake e-mail account in her husband's name and started sending Cassaday threatening and taunting messages.

And these manipulations worked. Within months, Cassaday had become so incensed that he was ready to do anything to liberate Sharee from the monster who had her in his grasp. Anything. Including murder.

On November 8, 1999, Sharee made a desperate call to her brother-in-law, Chuck, and told him that she was worried about Bruce. He was late coming home from work and he wasn't answering his phone. Since she was afraid to go down to the scrapyard after dark, she asked Chuck if he would check on his brother. Chuck, of course, said that he would. It would be he who found Bruce Miller's body, shotgunned to death among the wrecked cars that had been his livelihood.

Sharee was questioned about the shooting, of course, and suggested a name to the police. She said that she suspected a jealous former lover of being involved in the crime. The man was brought in and subjected to a polygraph, which he failed. However, there was no other evidence implicating him in the murder, and he was released. The police had, in any case, decided that Bruce Miller had probably been shot during a botched robbery.

Meanwhile, the newly-widowed Mrs. Miller appeared to be taking her husband's tragic death with remarkable fortitude. Just two days after Bruce was shot, she was seen dancing the night away at a bar in

Otisville, Michigan. Within two weeks, she had a live-in lover – and it wasn't Jerry Cassaday. Cassaday was about to learn in the cruelest possible way that he'd been taken for a fool. Almost immediately after Bruce's death, Sharee started distancing herself from him, either refusing to answer his messages or providing curt, hurtful responses. Then she told him that she had a new lover and started taunting him with the lurid details of the relationship. Finally, in December 1999, she told him never to contact her again.

Jerry was devastated by the betrayal, wracked with guilt over the murder he'd committed. He realized now that everything Sharee had told him had been a lie, that he'd been tricked into gunning down an innocent man. Eventually, it all became too much for him. On February 11, 2000, while living with relatives in Odessa, Missouri, Jerry Cassaday took his own life. His family found him slumped in a chair, a Bible open in his lap. He'd left behind three suicide notes. One of them was about to mete out some well-deserved justice to Sharee Miller.

The day after Cassaday's death, a relative was cleaning out the basement where he'd been staying when she came across a briefcase with an envelope taped to its lid. That envelope contained a confession to the murder of Bruce Miller and named Sharee as the instigator of the crime. Cassaday had also had the presence of mind to provide evidence that backed up his allegations. Inside the envelope was a hard copy of an online conversation he'd had with Sharee just hours before Bruce Miller was killed. In it, she'd provided him with directions to the salvage yard. She'd even sent him a reminder, telling him that it was time to go.

Sharee Miller's evil machinations had finally caught up with her. Once the details in Cassaday's note were verified, she was placed under arrest and charged with murder and conspiracy to commit murder. At her January 2001 trial, she was convicted on those charges and sentenced to 54 to 81 years.

But Sharee Miller wasn't about to let prison slow her down. She soon began corresponding with a man named Michael Denoyer and invited him to visit her. The two became engaged after their very first meeting.

In the meantime, Sharee's attorneys had taken her case on appeal. They would eventually succeed in getting her conviction quashed after a judge ruled that Jerry Cassaday's suicide note should never have been admitted into evidence. In July 2009, after spending more than 10 years behind bars, Sharee Miller was released on bond while she awaited her new trial.

Over the next three years, Sharee picked up her life as though nothing had happened. She partied, hung out in bars, and went through a succession of lovers. She also picked up her old habit of hanging out online, using a variety of social networks, her personal profiles littered with outrageous lies. Via these media, she frequently protested her innocence, writing with such persuasion that many believed her. In other posts, she admitted that she'd once led an immoral life but claimed that she was a changed woman, having found God in prison.

Those protestations would do her no good, however. When the matter eventually came to trial, the original conviction was affirmed, the original sentence reinstated. In August 2012, Sharee Miller was sent back to prison to serve out the remainder of her time. She did so still proclaiming a miscarriage of justice. Later, she'd have a change of heart.

In 2016, Miller addressed a four-page typed letter to Genesee Circuit Judge Judith Fullerton, admitting her role in her husband's death. She claimed that she could no longer live with the guilt of what she'd done. Given her history of lies and manipulation, there is probably a simpler reason behind her sudden candor. More than likely, she has begun entertaining thoughts of parole.

Rachel Wade

Josh Camacho was a strutting bantam of a little man. Standing just five-foot-five, and scrawny with it, Camacho was a 19-year-old high school dropout, frying chicken at a Chick-fil-A and still living at home with his parents. Nonetheless, he fancied himself as a tough guy. His Myspace page was littered with selfies, many of which featured him posing bare-chested, flexing his puny biceps and waving a gun in full gangsta mode. Camacho's other claim to fame in his hometown of Pinellas Park, Florida, was that he was a player, who always had several young women on the hook. This assertion at least had some validity. During the early months of 2009, when our story takes place, Camacho already had a child by one teenaged girl. Two others were vying for his affection in a rivalry that would grow increasingly fractious. Ultimately, it would end in murder.

The first of Camacho's warring harem was 19-year-old Rachel Wade. A Florida native, Rachel had grown up in a stable, loving home with her parents and younger brother. She was petite and pretty and blonde and had an outgoing personality that naturally drew people to her. Those same qualities would begin to get her into trouble as she entered her teens and started noticing (and being noticed by) teenaged boys. That was when she started rebelling, sneaking out of the house at night and staying out until all hours. At 15, she was picked up while having sex in a car with a 19-year-old, who was subsequently charged with statutory rape. Meanwhile, the situation in the Wade household had devolved into a battle of wills between Rachel and her parents. Several times the police were called to resolve domestic disputes. This situation would continue until Rachel dropped out of school, got a job waitressing at an Applebee's, and moved into her own apartment. By then, she was already dating Josh Camacho.

The relationship, however, was far from harmonious. Camacho often stayed over at Rachel's apartment, frequently sponged off her, and occasionally beat her up. He also sought to exert control over her life, telling her who she could associate with, what she could wear, and where she could go. He was particularly adamant that she should wear long pants at all times so that other boys couldn't ogle her legs. At the same time, he continued to sleep around, including with the mother of his child. The couple broke up repeatedly but always got back together again, with Rachel (despite being the injured party) usually doing the groveling. It was during one of their frequent splits that the third player in this melodrama arrived on the scene.

Like Rachel Wade, Sarah Ludeman had grown up in Pinellas Park. In fact, she'd lived all of her life just a short distance from Rachel, although the two girls had never met. Their proximity was just about the only thing they had in common. Where Rachel was petite, Sarah was big-boned, standing 5-foot-9 and weighing in at 166 pounds; where Rachael was a rebel, Sarah was a diligent student and close to her parents; where Rachael was promiscuous, Sarah was still a virgin at 18. In fact, she'd never even had a boyfriend until the day that she

walked into the Chick-fil-A and saw Josh Camacho. According to a
friend, who was with Sarah at the time, it was love at first sight.

To Sarah, inexperienced and blinded by love, Camacho appeared to
reciprocate those feelings. He flattered her, told her she was pretty,
paid her the kind of attention no boy had ever paid her before. Soon
she and Camacho were an item and she had surrendered her virginity
to him. That was when her parents started noticing a change in Sarah.
She was more argumentative, she started dressing differently, and
started listening to rap and hip hop, something she'd never enjoyed
before. More worryingly, she was regularly sporting bruises. They
feared that her new boyfriend was physically abusing her, but Sarah
denied this, saying she'd got the injuries while play fighting. Then she
dropped a bombshell, telling her parents that she no longer wanted to
study to be a veterinarian, something which had previously been a
burning ambition.

To Sarah's parents, it must have felt like they were losing their
daughter. They urged her to break things off with Camacho, but she
refused, saying that she loved him. Then the Ludemanns tried another
strategy, inviting Camacho to dinner at their house and trying to get to
know the young man their daughter had fallen for. They were left
perplexed by Sarah's choice. Camacho was a runt who stood a good
four inches shorter than Sarah. Moreover, he spoke, dressed and
carried himself like a pimp.

And, in a way, that is exactly what he was, a user and abuser of
gullible women. While Sarah was declaring her undying love for him,
Camacho was boasting to acquaintances that his relationship with her
was purely sexual. "Friends with benefits" was how he put it. He had

also started seeing Rachel Wade again and was back to staying over at her apartment. It was only a matter of time before the two women found out about each other. When they did, war was instantly declared.

It started after Sarah went on a trip to New York with Camacho and posted some photos on her Myspace page on her return. The pictures showed her and Camacho enjoying the sights of the Big Apple. One of them was captioned: "How do you like my new pictures? That's with my man, not yours." This was obviously aimed at Rachel, and she did not take long to respond; "I deserve so much better," she wrote on her page. That drew a sarcastic riposte from Sarah. "Oh, you think you can find better?" Rachel then somehow got hold of Sarah's cell phone number and left her an angry, profanity-laced message.

Thus were the battle lines drawn. Over the next few months, the taunts and threats flew back and forth, on MySpace and via text messages and voice mail. Then it spilled over into the physical world when Sarah started showing up at Rachel's place of work with a group of friends and started harassing her. They'd jostle her when she was carrying heavily-laden trays, call her names and generally give her a hard time. On one occasion, Sarah went to the Applebee's manager and complained that Rachel had spit in her food.

And where was Josh Camacho through all this? Loving every minute of it, that's where. He seemed to enjoy having the two women vying for his affection and even encouraged them to battle over him. "If you want to be with me, then you'll have to fight for me," he posted on his MySpace page. He could not have known how prophetic those words would be.

And so to the night of April 14, 2009, the night that all of the name calling, all of the verbal barbs and online sparring came to a head. Camacho had asked Rachel to hook up with him at his sister's house that evening, but he'd later sent her another message calling it off. He then sent a text to Sarah, asking her to come over and to bring some movies that they could watch together. Sarah said that she would. However, she could not resist the temptation of rubbing her victory in her rival's face. On the way to meet Camacho, she stopped outside Rachel's apartment, kept her hand on the horn of her vehicle for half a minute and then drove off.

This, according to Rachel Wade's later testimony, terrified her. She felt sure that Sarah would later return with her friends and attack her. She therefore called an ex-boyfriend, Javier Laboy, who suggested that she come over to his house in order to avoid a confrontation. Rachel said that she would, but as she was leaving her apartment, she made a fateful decision. She stopped in the kitchen, picked up a steak knife, and stuffed it into her purse.

Still, if Rachel had driven directly to Javier's home, if she'd spent the night there and allowed things to blow over, the story might have had a different ending. Instead, she made a stop at Camacho's house, to verify what she already suspected, that Camacho had blown her off for Sarah. Seeing Sarah's van parked outside, she instantly fired off a text to Camacho: "Now I know why you're not talking to me – because you have her."

"That's right," Camacho texted back. "I don't like you no more."

It was now 11 p.m. and Sarah Ludemann was already past her curfew. As she heard Rachel's vehicle driving away into the night, her phoned beeped, signaling a message. It was her father, asking when she'd be home. "Soon," Sarah messaged back, although she stayed another 45 minutes before telling Josh that she had to go. She was on her way out of the door when Josh's sister and her friend asked for a ride to McDonald's, which she agreed to. A short distance down the road, they encountered one of Sarah's friends who told her that she'd seen Rachel's car parked outside the house of a boy named Javier, just a few blocks away. Sarah then decided that she'd drive over there to confront her nemesis. As she raced in that direction, her cell phone rang. Recognizing the number, she switched to speaker. "I'm going to kill you!" Rachel shrieked down the line. "You and your Mexican boyfriend!"

Just moments later, Sarah screeched her car to a stop outside Javier's house. She spotted Rachel immediately, leaning against a car, talking to two boys. Then Sarah was out of her van, leaving the door flapping open behind her. She approached on the run, arms already flailing. She and her much smaller opponent then tangled, but only for a moment before Sarah reeled back, hand clutching her chest, blood oozing between her fingers. She then staggered towards her vehicle, only just making it before collapsing into the driver's seat. An autopsy would later reveal that she'd suffered two stab wounds, one to the shoulder and another which had penetrated her heart. She was dead before paramedics arrived.

Rachel Wade was taken into custody at the scene and transported to a police station for questioning. She made no attempt to deny stabbing Sarah but insisted that she had feared for her life and had acted in self-defense. Sarah had been harassing and threatening her for months, she said.

While this was undoubtedly true, it did not prevent Rachel from being charged with murder. At her trial, in August 2010, she continued her self-defense narrative but was damned by the many threatening messages she'd left on Sarah Ludemann's cell phone. "Your ass is mine," she'd said, "and I am guaranteeing you I am going to f**king murder you. I am letting you know that now. You're a f**king fat bitch, and I am going to f**king kill you, I swear on my life."

Given these hate-filled outbursts, it was hardly surprising when the jury returned a verdict of guilty to second-degree murder, taking just two-and-a-half hours to reach its decision. Rachel Wade was then sentenced to 27 years in prison, with a subsequent appeal affirming that sentence.

As for Josh Camacho, the "prize" over which these two young women had destroyed their lives, he was barred by Sarah's family from attending her funeral, and he left Pinellas Park soon after. He is believed to currently be living in New York City.

Harmohinder Sanghera

Sair Ali and Sana Ali were first cousins. They were also engaged to be married and had been since Sair was 17 and Sana was just nine years old. But aside from their upcoming betrothal, the pair's lifestyle could hardly have been more different. Sana had received a traditional Muslim upbringing in Pakistan; Sair had grown up in Bury, Greater Manchester, where his wealthy family owned a large detached house and he, at age 25, was already a successful businessman, the owner of a cellular phone company. He was also enjoying the other temptations that the western lifestyle had to offer. He was a regular at the area's nightclubs; he enjoyed a drink and was particularly fond of female company. It was on one of his nights out, in 2005, that he first encountered Harmohinder Kaur Sanghera.

Harmohinder, known as Mindy, was an accomplished young woman. At age 23, she was just a year away from graduating from Birmingham University's School of Dentistry. She already had a job lined up with one of Manchester's top dental practices. She was also a particularly attractive woman, one who immediately caught Sair Ali's roving eye. Despite the fact that she was Sikh and he Muslim (something that would have made a long-term relationship impossible between them) he homed in. Soon the pair were lovers, meeting for illicit liaisons at five-star hotels across the city.

For Ali, this was just another conquest, and he'd had plenty of those. But for Mindy, it was true love. She told him that she wanted to marry him and have his children. He responded that such an outcome was impossible due to their religious differences. In response, she said that she would convert to Islam. Although she had been, to that point, quite westernized and not particularly religious, she began to abstain from drinking alcohol, started wearing a headscarf, studying the Koran, and eating only halal food. Such was her devotion to the man she loved.

But what Mindy didn't know was that the issue of religion was a ruse. The real reason that Ali couldn't marry her was because he was already engaged. Ali had never told her about Sana, and Mindy remained blissfully unaware that she had a rival for Ali's affections.

This deception could not go on forever, of course. Sana had just turned 17. Half a world away in Pakistan, preparations were underway for an extravagant wedding. In December 2006, Ali traveled to the subcontinent and the first cousins became man and wife. Thereafter, Sana returned with her husband to the UK where she moved in with him at his family home.

For Sana, there was a massive adjustment to be made. A shy and unworldly teenager, she had never ventured out of her native land before. The gray skies and frigid January temperatures of Manchester must have been particularly unwelcoming, and it appeared to shrink her to less of a person than she'd been before. She seldom ventured out, had few friends, and spent most of her time at home, cooking and cleaning. She was, in fact, miserable and homesick, although she was too committed to her role as a wife to ever mention her unhappiness out loud.

Ali provided very little comfort to his child bride. His lifestyle had hardly changed at all. He continued his clubbing and womanizing and often arrived home in the early morning hours. He also appeared to have no sexual desire for his attractive, young wife. He'd failed to consummate the marriage on their wedding night and would later admit that when he did eventually have sex with Sana, it was with the help of Viagra. Despite his reticence, Sana had joyous news by the spring. She was pregnant with their first child.

Mindy, meanwhile, remained blissfully unaware of the pregnancy. She had learned of Ali's betrothal, but he'd told her that he'd married Sana out of a sense of duty, that he would have brought dishonor on his family had he failed to go through with it, that it was a loveless union. Mindy had accepted that, but she had started acting out in worryingly obsessive ways. She would keep a candle burning at all times that she and Ali were apart; she demanded that he phone her every night and speak to her until she fell asleep; she plagued him with texts, e-mails and letters. At other times, she spoke disparagingly of Sana, the rival whom she had never met. Often, she demanded to know whether Ali had had sex with his wife the night before. Whatever answer he gave would inevitably send her into a rage.

Other indicators were more troubling even than that. They pointed to a young woman undergoing a mental breakdown. "I think I am going crazy," Mindy wrote in one of her letters. "I thought I could handle it and deal with cutting contact with you but I can't. Maybe I am a psycho, crazy, or just a fool, or maybe all of those things."

The situation clearly needed a resolution, but the one that Ali chose only served to inflame an already volatile scenario. He proposed that he and Mindy enter into a Mutaa, a temporary Muslim "marriage." This, he believed, would provide Mindy with some sort of emotional stability while she underwent her final dentistry exams. The "marriage" would run until May 16, 2007, by which time Mindy would have completed her finals. Then perhaps they could sit down and talk things through sensibly. But the Mutaa would not run its full course. It would end five days early on May 11; it would end once Mindy found out that Sana Ali was eleven weeks pregnant.

Mindy was destroyed by the knowledge that the man she loved had fathered a child by another woman, even if that woman happened to be his wife. On the evening of Thursday, May 10, she spoke to Ali on the phone, tearfully declaring her love and telling him that she would not be able to go on without him. Ali, as he had always done, tried to appease her by telling her that he loved her, too, and by promising that the two of them would go away that weekend to talk things through. By the time he hung up the phone, he believed that he had bought himself some time in which to worm himself out of a tricky situation. He was dead wrong.

The following day, while the rest of the Ali family was worshiping at a nearby mosque, Sana Ali answered a knock at the door. The attractive young woman who stood there introduced herself as a friend of the family, and Sana, therefore, allowed her in to wait for their return.

Then the woman asked for a tour of the house, and Sana was happy to oblige her. It was in the bedroom that Sana shared with her husband that the guest struck. Mindy had brought a six-and-a-half-inch kitchen knife with her to the Ali residence. Now she drew it and launched a frenzied attack on her young victim. Blow after blow rained down on the helpless Sana, reducing her to a bloody, convulsing mess on the floor. Then, as the teenager's life ebbed away, Mindy raised her top and plunged the blade repeatedly into her slightly bulging belly. Then she fled. Sana was discovered by the Ali family when they returned from the mosque. By then, both she and her unborn child were long dead.

Questioned by the police, Ali had no option but to confess to his longstanding affair with Mindy and to admit that she was the only one with a motive to kill his wife. Mindy was taken into custody that same day and admitted that she had visited Sana at the Ali home. However, she insisted that Sana had been alive and well when she'd left. According to her, she'd only called on Sana to inform her that her husband was a cheat.

Harmohinder Sanghera would carry this same story into the trial, with her defense team suggesting that it was actually Ali who'd killed his wife in order to free himself from a loveless marriage. Ali tearfully denied this on the stand, insisting that he'd loved Sana, that he'd been looking forward to married life and fatherhood and that he'd been trying to break things off with the defendant. The defense, in response, labeled him a liar.

But the jilted lover narrative was the one that was ultimately accepted by the jury. Mindy Sanghera was found guilty of murder and sentenced to life in prison, with a minimum term of 14 years. Ali also did not escape the ire of the judge. He was described as "weak-willed and reprehensible" during the summation.

In the aftermath of the trial, Sair Ali left the UK to begin a new life elsewhere. Harmohinder Sanghera, meanwhile, will spend just 14 years behind bars for the savage slaying of a blameless young girl and her unborn baby. That seems a paltry price to pay for snuffing out two innocent lives.

Eva Coo

The Great Depression was a dark era in American history, a time of want and deprivation, of soup kitchens and work queues and millions of desperate, shiftless people trying to eke out a meager living. And yet, as with all such calamities, there were those who thrived in adversity. One of those individuals was Eva Coo, a boisterous, strongly-built woman who ran a bar in upstate New York during the 1920s and '30s. While most of her fellow citizens struggled to keep body and soul together, Eva began with nothing and built up a thriving business, bought several properties and owned three automobiles. Regrettably, she also ended up on the wrong side of the law.

Born in Haliburton, Ontario in 1894, Eva Curry grew to be a precocious girl who eloped with a rail worker named William Coo while she was still in her teens. The pair traveled to Toronto and married there, although the union would last only a few years before Eva walked out on her husband. She next ended up in Oneonta, a small city in Otsego County, New York, arriving in 1921 with not much more than the clothes in her suitcase. Eva, however, would not remain so for long. She was an ambitious woman with a strong work ethic.

This was, of course, the age of prohibition, and she saw opportunity in that. Before long, she'd set up an illegal speakeasy which she called Eva's Place.

With her naturally outgoing personality, Eva made the perfect hostess. She'd also chosen the ideal location to set up shop. Oneonta was, at the time, a bustling railroad town, a junction for all points east and west. Rail commuters with an hour or two to spare invariably ended up spending that time at Eva's Place. There they rubbed shoulders with Eva's regular clientele – truck drivers, railroad employees, and construction workers, even cops and local politicians. As the business thrived, Eva took on several employees, including a number of "hostesses" whose job it was to socialize with the clientele and get them to empty their wallets. One of these was a 27-year-old mother-of-two from Pennsylvania named Martha Clift. Martha began working at Eva's Place in 1933, and people soon noticed that she and her employer were as thick as thieves.

The third player in the sordid drama that was about to unfold was also an employee of Eva's. Harry "Gimpy" Wright had once been a farmer, but an accident had left him partially disabled and unable to care for himself. After his mother died in 1931, Harry had sold the farm and moved to Oneonta, where he became a regular at Eva's Place. Despite his disability, the 52-year-old was a heavy drinker and an incorrigible womanizer. He would often leave the bar in the early morning hours, barely able to walk. He'd then stagger off along Route 7, often passing out along the roadside. It was a minor miracle that he was never struck by a car during these drunken rambles.

Gimpy did have one redeeming feature, though, at least in Eva Coo's mind. He had a sizeable nest egg from his inheritance and the sale of his farm. Before long, Eva had struck up a deal with him. In exchange for a lump sum payment of $2,000, she would take responsibility for his care. Harry could sleep at the tavern and would be a full-time employee, working as a handyman. He'd get his meals cooked and his laundry done, and there would always be someone at hand in case of a medical emergency. To Harry, it must have sounded like a fair proposition because he handed over the money soon after.

Harry Wright would be a familiar face at Eva's Place for over two years. But on the morning of June 14, 1934, an apparently concerned Eva called the local police and reported that her handyman was missing. According to Eva, Gimpy had staggered out of the bar the previous evening and hadn't been seen since. She was worried that he may have come to harm.

A search was immediately launched for the missing man. And it didn't take long before it was tragically resolved. Harry's mangled corpse was found lying in a roadside ditch along Route 7, about a half-mile from Eva's Place. It appeared that his luck had finally run out, that he'd stumbled into the road and been hit by a passing vehicle. That, at least, was the verdict of the local coroner who ruled the death accidental. The body was then dispatched to a funeral parlor to be prepared for burial.

But here things began to take a turn for the unusual. Years earlier, Harry had purchased a plot at the local cemetery, complete with headstone. But while that plot was being prepared to receive him to his eternal rest, cemetery workers noticed that the headstone had been tampered with. Specifically, Harry's date of birth had been chiseled away. That peculiar act of vandalism would soon be explained when the Oneonta police got a call from a representative of the Met Life Insurance Company. Someone had lodged a claim against an insurance policy taken on Harry Wright's life. That someone was Eva Coo.

Two things did not sit right with the insurer. First, Coo was not a blood relative of the deceased; second, Wright's age had been understated on the policy, probably with the intent of lowering the premiums. The police agreed that those irregularities were cause for concern. Now the defaced headstone made sense. Someone had obviously wanted to hide Wright's true date of birth. And since only one person would benefit from such an act, it did not take a genius to work out who was responsible.

Eva Coo was brought in for questioning. In the interim, the police had received another puzzling piece of information. On the night that Gimpy Wright died, a family living on a farm near Crumhorn Mountain had reported that two women had parked a car on their property. The women had been asked to leave, and they eventually had, but the family had reported the incident anyway. They were also able to identify the trespassers. One was Eva Coo; the other was Martha Clift. What, investigators wondered, had they been doing out in the middle of nowhere, in the middle of the night? And why had they not mentioned this strange excursion before? In order to get the answers to those questions, investigators decided to bring in Martha Clift to be questioned alongside her friend and employer. It did not take long before she was talking.

According to Clift, Eva had paid her $200 to help her murder Harry Wright. On the night in question, Eva had waited until Wright was falling down drunk and then loaded him into a car. The three of them had driven to Crumhorn Mountain where Eva had struck Harry on the head with a mallet. After he collapsed, Martha had driven over him with the car, then backed up and driven over him again. She'd done this on Eva's instructions, she said.

Originally, Eva had intended leaving Harry's body where it fell. But they'd been interrupted by the landholders and had, therefore, loaded up Harry's corpse and driven it to a spot closer to the tavern, where it would later be found. Confronted with these allegations, Eva eventually confessed to the murder, although she insisted that the mallet blow could not have killed Harry and it was being hit by the car that actually ended his life. Either way, both women were going on trial for murder. Before that trial had even begun, there was further bad news for Eva. The state had decided to offer Martha a deal. She was allowed to plead to second degree murder in exchange for her testimony against her employer.

The trial of Eva Coo took place in Cooperstown, New York, during August 1934. It was one of the media sensations of the day, with huge crowds gathering outside the courthouse. Some entrepreneurial individuals had even crafted souvenirs and memorabilia of the event and walked among the masses hawking their wares. The press, meanwhile, covered the event with sensationalized stories about the so-called "Mallet Killer." These were invariably low on fact and high on melodrama.

Against this background, Eva Coo never stood a chance. And once her co-accused took the stand to point her out as the mastermind behind the murder-for-profit scheme, she was doomed. In the end, it took the jury just one hour to return a guilty verdict. Coo was then sentenced to death while Martha Clift got 20 years.

On the same day that she received her sentence, Eva Coo was transported to Sing Sing to await execution. There were appeals, of course, but, in truth, Coo did not receive adequate representation; her lawyers merely going through the motions. They raised no objection, for example, regarding the extraordinary circumstances under which their client's confession had been extracted. It would later be revealed that the Sheriff had exhumed Harry Wright's body and brought it into the room where Coo was being interrogated. There, the rotting corpse was removed from its coffin and placed in front of the suspect, who nearly gagged on the noxious fumes coming off the cadaver. Given this unconventional interrogation tactic, it is no surprise that Coo almost immediately started talking.

And yet, her lawyer had not raised the issue at trial, had made no attempt to have the confession suppressed. In fact, he barely spoke to his client while she was on death row, although he did phone the warder to reserve four seats at her execution.

On June 27, 1935, Eva Coo was informed that her clemency appeal to Governor Herbert Lehman had been refused. At 11:00 p.m. that night, she was brought to the death chamber and escorted to the electric chair. She appeared tense, but nonetheless maintained her composure, walking erect and with her shoulders pushed back. "Goodbye, darlings!" she said to her female warders as the straps were fastened around her wrists and ankles. Several minutes later, after receiving two jolts of electricity, she was dead. Eva Coo was the third woman to be put to death at Sing Sing during the 20th century.

Barbara Dalton

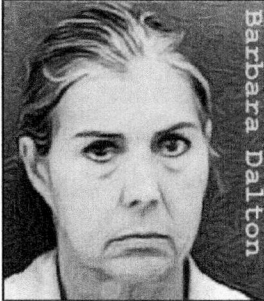

Heartbreak is something we all have to deal with at some time in our lives. We meet someone and fall in love and then, over time, we realize that the relationship isn't going to work, that the feelings of our beloved are not as intense as those we are experiencing. Then comes the dreaded "it's not you, it's me" conversation, and we are cut loose to bury ourselves in self-pity and endless tubs of Ben and Jerry's. Usually, though, we survive, we get on with our lives and move on to other things, other relationships. That is the way life works for most people. Barbara Dalton did not follow the template.

Barbara Dalton and Mark Sullivan had been involved in a 14-year relationship, a romance that had been brought to an end in May 2001 when Mark admitted to Barbara that he no longer had feelings for her. Shortly thereafter, he'd moved his stuff out of the house they'd bought together in Mansfield, Georgia. Before long, he was dating again and was living with his new love, a single mom named Donna Sanders. Barbara, too, appeared to have put the past behind her. She'd started a rebound romance with a man named Joe Waters who she described as the love of her life.

But there were signs, worrying signs, that Barbara had not really moved on. On one occasion, while taking her mother to a favorite restaurant, she made a considerable detour just to pass by Donna Sanders's house. She then pointed it out to her mother as "the house where Mark is now living with that woman." And an even more troubling incident occurred soon after, when Barbara confronted Mark at his parents' home and pulled a gun on him. She threatened to shoot him if he did not drop a lawsuit he'd launched over his half of their shared property. Mark agreed to do so and even drove with Barbara to his lawyer's office. But he later managed to get away from her and call 911. Barbara was then arrested, although she was later released without charge. That should have been a warning.

On the afternoon of May 23, 2002, 10-year-old Wesley Sanders stepped off the school bus at his home on Dixie Road in Mansfield. This was part of the boy's daily routine, and he knew that he'd be home alone for a short while before his mother returned from work. Except that, today, he wasn't alone. There was a woman standing in the drive, a woman he didn't recognize. She seemed friendly enough, though, and he figured she was probably a friend of his mother's. When she asked if he would hide with her in the backyard, so that they could surprise his mom when she got home, Wesley agreed.

When Donna Sanders did arrive, however, she seemed less than pleased to see the unannounced visitor. Nonetheless, Donna allowed the woman into the house where they stood in the kitchen and conducted a terse conversation. Feeling uncomfortable with the situation, Wesley retreated to his room and remained there until his mother called out to him. Then he, his mom, and the stranger got into his mother's Ford F-150 truck. They started driving, heading down

Tabernacle Cemetery Road until the woman told his mom to stop. Then she ordered them out of the truck, and it was then that he noticed that the woman (who his mother referred to as Barbara) was holding a gun in her hand. "Don't shoot me in front of my boy," Donna begged the woman. For one terrifying moment, Wesley thought that she was going to shoot them both.

But Barbara didn't fire. Instead she ordered them back into the truck, this time with her at the wheel. They then headed back into Mansfield, stopping at a house Wesley didn't recognize. Although he didn't know it at the time, this was the home of Barbara's 23-year-old son, Brian Dean.

Brian was surprised by his mother's arrival and concerned by her demeanor. He did not know the woman and the boy she'd arrived with, but Barbara introduced the woman to him as "the woman Mark has been living with for the last couple of months." She then asked him to tell some friends (who were visiting) to leave, saying that they needed to speak privately. Once those friends had departed, Brian grabbed his mother and demanded to know what was going on. "You haven't done anything crazy or stupid, have you?" he asked, to which she responded, "No, we're just here to talk."

But Brian had seen enough. The woman and the boy were quite clearly terrified and were certainly there under duress. Well, that ended now. He leaned across the coffee table reaching for the car keys, wanting to hand them to the woman. That was when his mother produced a .38 from her waistband, pointed it and fired. A single shot reverberated across the living room. Before Brian even had a chance to react, his mother's reluctant guest lay slumped in the chair, a bullet hole perforating her forehead.

Brian Dean would later describe the chaotic aftermath of the shooting in court. He said that his mother had given no indication of her intention, that she simply drew the weapon and fired in one fluid movement. Then she bolted from the room, not even checking whether her bullet had found its mark. Brian was on the move, too. He immediately snatched up the little boy and made a run for it. Moments later, he was banging on his neighbor's door, then dialing 911 and telling his harrowing story. By the time the police arrived, Barbara Dalton was gone. She'd fled the scene in her victim's truck.

Meanwhile, in the nearby town of Covington, Mark Sullivan was getting anxious. He and Donna had made an appointment at a tanning salon that afternoon, but she hadn't shown. She also was not answering her phone, and that was unusual. Donna was the most reliable person he'd ever met. Eventually, Mark decided to drive home to check on her. He was heading down County Road 213 when he spotted her truck driving in the opposite direction at high speed. Only it wasn't Donna at the wheel, it was Barbara. Seriously concerned now, Mark looked for a place to turn around. By the time he was able to do so, the truck was long gone. That was when his phone jangled into life. It was Brian, Barbara's son, and he had a terrible tale to tell.

Barbara Dalton was taken into custody that same day. At her trial, in mid-2004, the prosecutor made clear his intention of seeking the death penalty. The case certainly warranted that consideration since the murder had been committed during the commission of another crime (kidnapping) and appeared to have been premeditated. The issue of wantonness also applied. What could be more wanton than gunning down a mother in front of her 10-year-old son?

And there was also no way that Dalton could deny culpability. Even her own son appeared as a prosecution witness. All she could do was to fall back on a familiar excuse for accused murderers the world over. She said that she didn't remember.

According to Barbara, the murder had not been motivated by jealousy since she had "no feelings" for Mark Sullivan. It was she who had ended the relationship, she insisted. She said that she'd gone to Donna's house that day to discuss the ongoing property dispute she'd been having with Mark. She had then persuaded Donna to accompany her to her son's house because she wanted his advice on the matter. She recalled arriving there and introducing Donna and Wesley to her son and his friends. After that, everything was a blank.

Unfortunately for Barbara, there were others with a far better recall of the day's events than she. Wesley Sanders had refused to discuss the actual shooting (or perhaps he'd simply shut out the memory of his mother's murder), but he had provided a counselor with a detailed description of the incidents leading up to the horrific event. That statement left no doubt as to Dalton's intentions. Once it was read out in court, there could only be one outcome.

Barbara Dalton was found guilty of first-degree murder in July 2004. But the prosecutor did not get the sentence he'd hoped for with the jury deciding that there was reasonable doubt as to the death penalty conditions. Dalton was sentenced instead to life in prison. She is ineligible for parole.

Kimberly McCarthy

Kimberly Lagayle McCarthy was not the kind of woman whose path you'd want to cross. Once, she'd been a more or less law-abiding citizen, a high school graduate earning her living as a home healthcare therapist. But then the demon of crack cocaine had entered her life, and everything had changed. She'd lost her job, her marriage had disintegrated, she'd been convicted on a charge of forgery and spent time in prison. And that was only a foretaste of what was to come. Soon she'd resort to the ultimate sin to service her need. She'd resort to murder. In fact, Kimberly McCarthy may well be a serial killer.

The murder that would catapult McCarthy into the national headlines was a particularly savage one. It happened in Lancaster, Texas, on the night of July 21, 1997. On that evening, McCarthy had phoned her neighbor, 71-year-old retired psychology professor Dorothy Booth, and asked if she could come over to borrow a cup of sugar. The professor had, of course, said yes. Moments later, McCarthy was at her door, all sweetness and light until she was inside the apartment. Then, without warning, she attacked, using a large kitchen knife that she had brought with her.

Professor Booth was cut down before she even had a chance to react. She was slashed and stabbed, suffering five deep wounds before she was bludgeoned into submission with a brass candlestick holder. Then, as the elderly woman lay bleeding to death on the floor, McCarthy tried to wrench her wedding ring from her finger. Unable to do so, she used the knife to hack the finger from her still-living victim's hand. She then pocketed Professor Booth's purse and car keys and drove away from the scene in the professor's Mercedes station wagon.

McCarthy didn't go far, just to a local liquor store where she used her victim's credit card to buy some booze. Her next stop was at a pawn shop, where she exchanged the stolen wedding ring for $200. With cash in hand, she drove to a crack house. There she handed over the car keys to a dealer. "I need some crack bad," she told him. "Give me a bump or something."

By now, Professor Booth's brutalized body had been discovered, and it did not take the police long to zero in on a suspect. This was not a cleverly thought-out crime, nor had it been carried out in a way that would make the killer difficult to uncover. McCarthy was soon in custody, arrested with the victim's purse still in her possession. Despite this, she denied that she'd done anything wrong. She blamed the murder on a couple of drug dealers named 'Kilo' and 'J.C.,' who she claimed to have met in South Dallas. But the Dallas police had a reliable and well-established network of informants within the local drug scene, and none of them had ever heard of these men. In any case, forensic evidence was about to point the finger directly at Kimberly McCarthy.

After McCarthy was arrested on July 22, 1997, investigators obtained a search warrant for her residence. There they found smears of blood on several surfaces, most pertinently on a 10-inch butcher knife that matched the stab wounds to the victim's body. The knife itself had been thoroughly cleaned, but blood had seeped in under the handle, and once that was removed, the police had a sufficient amount for a DNA test. It matched Professor Dorothy Booth.

Yet even with this overwhelming evidence against her, Kimberly McCarthy continued to insist that she was innocent. The matter went to trial in November 1998, where she entered a not guilty plea but was nonetheless convicted, with the jury recommending that she be put to death. That judgement would be overturned in 2001 after an appeals court ruled that McCarthy's rights were violated when the Dallas Police Department obtained a written statement from her after she had asked to talk to a lawyer. That meant that the prosecution had to prove its case all over again at a new trial. Fortunately, they still had strong forensics to make their case for them.

On October 20, 2002, Kimberly McCarthy was again convicted of capital murder, with the jury taking just an hour to come to its guilty verdict. The sentence of the court was again death by lethal injection, and again there was an appeal. This time, the defense cited racial bias based on the make-up of the jury which had included just one African-American. However, since no objection had been raised at the actual trial, this appeal was dismissed. Kimberly McCarthy was returned to death row. As things stood, she would become only the fourth woman executed by the state of Texas since the reinstatement of the death penalty in 1976. During that same period, 496 convicted male killers had been put to death by the state.

But before that execution could be carried out, there was a significant twist in the tale. Kimberly McCarthy was indicted on two more counts of murder, bringing her death toll to three and marking her out as a serial killer. The victims in these murders were also elderly women, both killed in December 1988. Maggie Harding, 81, had been stabbed and then clubbed to death with a meat tenderizing mallet; 85-year-old Jettie Lucas had been beaten with a claw hammer and savagely stabbed. McCarthy would never stand trial for these crimes since she was already on death row awaiting execution.

What was particularly significant in these murders was the profile of the victims. While in prison, McCarthy and her supporters had been making a lot of noise about the discriminatory nature of her conviction. They claimed that she'd only been sentenced to death because she was black and her victim was white. But Maggie Harding and Jettie Lucas were both African-Americans, giving a lie to this assertion. In fact, Harding and Lucas were both friends of McCarthy's mother. Her only basis for choosing them as victims appeared to be their possession of cash or saleable assets and their inability to defend themselves. Standing between Kimberly McCarthy and a hit on the crack pipe was a dangerous, indeed deadly, place to be.

But McCarthy would never hurt another innocent victim. Her appeals exhausted, she was brought to the death chamber at the Texas State Penitentiary in Huntsville on June 26, 2013. There she was strapped to a gurney and an intravenous tube was inserted into her arm. "This is not a loss. This is a win," she said in her final statement. "I'm going home to be with Jesus." Then, as the single lethal dose of pentobarbital began to flow, she uttered: "God is great." Moments later, she took several loud, raspy breaths and then fell silent, although her breathing continued for a minute more before it stopped. She was pronounced dead at 6:37 p.m.

Kelly Fuller

Kelly Fuller was a high-maintenance girlfriend, jealous, possessive, and constantly demanding of attention. For Mike Bloom, it was doubly difficult having her around. Mike was 19 years old and working as a DJ at a roller-skating rink in Perth, Australia, a job that attracted many teenaged girls to him. At first, Kelly had been okay with this, willing to accept Mike's assurances that it was only her that he was interested in. But all too soon, her obsessive side emerged. She became ever more clingy, plaguing Mike with phone calls, wanting to know what he was doing at all hours of the day. She also accused him of sleeping with any girl he so much as exchanged the time of day with. Eventually, her jealous rants became too much for Mike. He called time on the relationship.

But breaking up with someone like Kelly Fuller was never going to be that easy. When Mike told her that it was over between them, she insisted that it wasn't and then proceeded to trash his studio, destroying records and DJ equipment. She then began stalking Mike, calling and messaging him, showing up at his place of work, intimidating any girl who got close to him. If that was an effort to win back Mike's affections, it failed dismally, serving only to alienate him even more. In any case, he now had a new love interest, 15-year-old Jessica Lang.

Jessica was young and blonde and pretty. She was also a level-headed young woman. To her, the flirtation with Mike Lang was no more than a distraction. Sure, Mike was cool, and glib, and fun to be with, but Jessica had bigger plans for her life. She wanted to train as a hairdresser and had been accepted for an apprenticeship in the new

year, after she finished school. Not that any of that mattered to Kelly
Fuller. To her, Jessica was an obstacle to her happiness. She naively
believed that Mike would return to her if Jessica were out of the way.
And so she decided to do just that – to remove Jessica from the
picture.

On the rainy spring day of September 24, 1998, 18-year-old Kelly
Fuller slipped one of her father's fishing knives into her handbag, put
on a pair of gloves, and set off for the home of her rival, in the Perth
suburb of Bicton. Jessica was home alone and somewhat surprised
when she answered the doorbell and found Kelly on her porch. Her
initial instinct was to slam the door in her face, but Kelly said she just
wanted to talk and seemed so distraught that Jessica took pity on her.
Leaving the door ajar, she turned around and walked back into the
house. That was a fatal mistake.

Jessica had just reached the end of the hall when Kelly struck. The first
blow caught the 15-year-old in the neck, the razor-sharp fish knife
slicing easily through flesh and nicking the carotid. That alone, would
have been fatal, but it was only the beginning of Kelly Fuller's
onslaught. As her rival slid to the floor, Kelly was on her, stabbing and
slashing with the knife, most of the thrusts aimed at the head and neck,
causing horrendous damage. Jessica begged for mercy, but Kelly was
caught in the midst of a homicidal frenzy. She did not stop stabbing
until 47 wounds had been inflicted and Jessica lay dead at her feet.
Then Kelly went to the bathroom and washed the blood from her
hands. Her bloodstained clothes were concealed under a raincoat. On
her way out, she tossed a brick through a window to make it look as
though Jessica had been killed by an intruder.

It was Jessica's father, John, who had the horrible misfortune of discovering his daughter's butchered corpse. He immediately called 000, bringing police and paramedics racing to the suburban home. The latter, unfortunately, were superfluous. Jessica was already dead. Now it was up to the police to track down her killer and bring him or her to justice.

Was it ever likely that Kelly would get away with this crudely executed crime? No, she would inevitably have come under suspicion once detectives questioned her friends and her former boyfriend. Everyone knew that she was obsessed with Mike and that she hated Jessica. But Kelly made it easy for the police. Rather than keeping her horrible deed to herself, she involved someone else in the murder.

Remy Bridger was a close friend of Kelly Fuller. It was to her that Kelly had turned after her breakup with Mike Bloom. During her frequent rants about Mike and his new girlfriend, Kelly had often threatened to kill Jessica, but Remy had never taken her seriously. Now she had reason to rethink her incredulity. After returning home, Kelly had taken a shower and tossed her bloodstained clothes into the washing machine. She'd then called Remy and asked her to come over. Remy had listened in amazement as Kelly had described the murder and shown her the knife that had ended Jessica Lang's life. "I need to get rid of it," she'd said. "Want to help?"

Of course, Remy said yes. She was hardly going to refuse when Kelly was standing right in front of her, holding the blade that had just snuffed out another young woman's life. And so, she accompanied Kelly to a storm drain, where Kelly tossed in the murder weapon, wrapped in a tea towel. Later, the two women visited a Freemantle shopping mall, a trip that took them past the Lang residence. Noting the lack of activity at the house, Kelly commented that Jessica had probably not been found yet. It was then that Remy knew what needed to be done. As soon as she was free of her friend, she called the police and told them what she knew. Kelly was arrested that same day.

Kelly Fuller went on trial at the West Australian Supreme Court in 1999. She entered a not guilty plea to willful murder, with her lawyer arguing that she had not gone to the Lang residence intent on murder. The evidence, however, said different. If Fuller had not planned on killing Jessica, why had she been carrying a knife? Why had she been wearing gloves on a clammy spring day?

Those unanswered questions were enough to convince the jurors that this was indeed a case of premeditated murder. They found Kelly Fuller guilty. The mandatory sentence was life in prison, although the judge was somewhat lenient in setting the minimum term at just 11 years. That was a shorter period than Jessica Lang had been allowed to live on this earth. Kelly Fuller is currently incarcerated at Bandyup Women's Prison.

Maria Helena Lee

Maria Lee was a supreme predator, as deadly as the savanna cats that her homeland of South Africa is famous for. Except in Lee's case, the prey was gullible young men who she lured in, chewed up and spat out when she was done with them. Most survived with no more than a broken heart and shattered illusions of love. For one man, though, there would be no escape. His attraction to the femme fatale would cost him his life.

Maria Helena Gertruida van Niekerk was born in 1899 and grew up in the Lichtenburg district of the Transvaal. She married young, tying the knot with a man named Oosterhuizen when she was just 16. The couple would have four sons, but they divorced in 1929 over allegations of infidelity. Thereafter, Maria married a man named Kruger, but that union lasted just a few months. In 1934, the now 35-year-old Maria was wed for a third time. Her new husband was called Jan de Klerk Lee, a metal worker who was eleven years her junior. Shortly after the wedding, they set up home in Pretoria where they started a small construction business. But Jan Lee was not long for this world. He died of tuberculosis in March of 1941, leaving his widow an estate worth around £3000, a considerable sum in those days.

In the modern parlance, we would probably call Maria Lee a cougar, an attractive, middle-aged widow with money and an insatiable appetite for younger men. During the Second World War, she corresponded with a number of soldiers who were at the time serving in the North African campaign, writing titillating letters that hinted at carnal delights on their return from the war. One of those men, 23-year-old Private Alwyn Smith, took these promises quite literally. When the war ended and he was discharged from the military, Smith traveled to Pretoria where he contacted Maria. The two of them met for tea at Polley's Hotel, but Maria had bad tidings for her young suitor. She was moving to Cape Town. Her train ticket was booked for the next day.

Smith was clearly disappointed by the news. But he was also determined. As Maria sat in her carriage the next morning, he suddenly appeared in the doorway. He, too, had decided to move south. The couple were inseparable for the rest of the journey. They arrived in the Cape on October 13, 1945. There, they got a room together in a boarding house, living as man and wife. Soon after, Maria got a job at the pharmaceutical firm, Lennon's. Now 45 years old, she had claimed on her application that she was a war widow, aged 29. She still looked youthful enough to pull it off. She also did not look out of place beside her young beau.

But already storm clouds were gathering over the relationship. Smith was pressing Maria to marry him, and Maria was stalling. The reason for her indecision was this – she had promised herself to a man named

C.J. Olivier, another of the soldiers that she had corresponded with
during the war. Maria had never actually met Olivier, but they had
discussed marriage in their letters, and she considered herself engaged
to him. Moreover, Olivier had far better prospects than Alwyn Smith.
He owned a farm in the Orange Free State and was quite wealthy.
Alwyn was more or less penniless. In fact, he was always borrowing
money from Maria on some pretense or other.

And so, Maria privately came to a decision. She was going to dump
Alwyn Smith and marry C.J. Olivier. She did not, however, want to
hurt Alwyn's feelings. Actually, she was quite fond of him. And so she
continued stringing him along, even accepted a proposal of marriage.
Then, while Smith was out of town, she packed up her stuff and left,
traveling to Bethlehem in the Orange Free State to marry her wealthy
farmer. The marriage, however, was short-lived. Within months, Maria
was back in Cape Town, a divorcee yet again. Despite her desertion,
Alwyn welcomed her back with open arms.

By now, Maria had come to the conclusion that Alwyn Smith was
probably the man for her. He might not be a reliable breadwinner, but
he had proven his loyalty. The problem was that Smith was still
pressing her to marry him and, after four failures in the matrimonial
arena, Maria wasn't sure that she wanted to tread that path again.
Then, just as she was softening her stance on the issue, she received
tragic news. Her mother had died. Maria was devastated by the death
and quite naturally turned to her lover for solace. But she found Alwyn
strangely unsympathetic. "Your mother was old," he said. "Everyone
dies. Get over it."

Those ill-judged words would put a strain on the relationship. So much so that Smith eventually told Maria that it was over between them. He then decamped for Durban where he remained for several months before returning to Maria's side again. But things had changed between them. Smith was drinking heavily and he was gambling, borrowing money all over town to fund his habit. Maria also suspected that he might be stealing from her. Often, their landlady would hear them arguing in their room, usually over money, although sometimes there was mention of stolen jewelry.

This particular comment related to an incident that had happened while Maria was working for the American Swiss jewelry company. Several thousand pounds' worth of merchandise had gone missing, and Maria had been suspected. Her employer had had no proof to incriminate her and so no charges were brought. She had, however, been forced to resign.

We will never know for sure whether Maria was responsible for the theft. What we do know is that Alwyn Smith believed that she was guilty and was now using that to wheedle money out of her. He threatened to go to the police unless she kept funding his gambling habit. That was, in retrospect, not the smartest move he ever made.

In December 1946, Alwyn Smith started complaining of stomach cramps. He was also frequently nauseous and prone to bouts of diarrhea. Over the next two months, his condition deteriorated to such an extent that Maria's landlady urged her to call a doctor. Dr. Morris Helman was duly summoned on March 13, 1947, and prescribed a tonic which seemed to alleviate the symptoms. The respite, however, was brief. When Dr. Helman was called again, a week later, he found the patient in a worse condition than before. Smith had a rash all over his body, he was retching continuously, he complained of acute stomach pains. On 22 March, Dr. Helman ordered that he be admitted to hospital. Helman suspected that Smith might be suffering from scarlet fever.

Tests for that disease would prove negative. Nonetheless, the hospital stay proved to be hugely beneficial. Smith's condition quickly improved. Within a week, he was ready to be discharged. He walked from the hospital a healthy man, straight into the arms of his loving fiancée. One week later, Dr. Helman was again summoned and found his patient as before, sweating, vomiting, and rolling around in his bed from the excruciating pains in his stomach. The doctor immediately suggested that he be readmitted to the hospital, but both Smith and Lee refused, saying that they had lost faith in the medical profession and would prefer to rely on bed rest and homeopathy. Unable to convince them otherwise, Dr. Helman left.

Alwyn Smith would hover in this hellish condition for nearly a month, all the while attended by Maria Lee. On May 2, Dr. Helman received a telephone call from Lee, saying that she believed that Smith was dying. She wanted the doctor present so that he could issue a death certificate. But Smith was still alive when Helman got there, and this time the doctor formed a different opinion of his condition. He decided that Smith was suffering from arsenic poisoning. Since such a diagnosis has serious implications, Helman called a colleague of his, Dr. Philip Leftwich, a specialist in such cases. After examining the patient, Leftwich concurred. Smith had ingested arsenic. Over the protests of Maria Lee, he ordered immediate transportation to a hospital. It was already too late. Alwyn Smith died within an hour of arrival.

This was now a matter for the police, and the main question they needed answered was whether Alwyn Smith's death was accident, suicide, or murder. First, though, the diagnosis of arsenic poisoning had to be confirmed. That would require an autopsy, which was conducted by Professor E.N. Keen of the University of Cape Town's Anatomy School. Keen found traces of arsenic in all the major organs and also in Smith's hair, suggesting that he had ingested the poison over a protracted period. The fatal dose, according to Keen's report, had been administered within 24 hours of death.

The obvious suspect was Maria Lee. Not only had she and the victim fought constantly during their final months together, but it was found that there was an insurance policy on Smith's life, with Lee the sole beneficiary. She stood to gain £3000 from his demise. But what the police lacked was a smoking gun. There was no evidence that Lee had ever purchased arsenic, and a search of her room turned up nothing that would incriminate her. For a time, it appeared that Lee had gotten away with murder. She was even allowed to leave Cape Town, to move back to Pretoria where she hoped to put the tragedy behind her and start a new life. It wasn't until September 1947 that a warrant was issued for her arrest.

In truth, the police had very little evidence against Lee. Had she held her nerve, there is every chance that she would have been acquitted at trial. But Lee did not hold her nerve. She decided to concoct a cover story to back up her version of events – that Smith had killed himself by consuming an arsenic-based ant poison. In order to do that, she recruited her cellmate, a woman named Margrieta Minaar.

What Lee wanted from Minaar was this. She was to testify that she had known Alwyn Smith during the months that he was living in Durban. She was further to say that he was frequently ill during that time, with symptoms similar to those he had displayed before his death. The implication was that Smith had already started taking the poison while he was in Durban and had continued to do so after he returned to Cape Town. In exchange for her help, Lee would get a friend of hers to pay Minaar's £50 bail. She would also pay an additional £100 in "expenses." Minaar agreed to the deal. Then she promptly reneged and told her story to the police instead.

Maria Lee was committed for trial at the Cape Town High Court in April 1948. By then, the case had become a national sensation, and there were long queues for the public gallery. The defendant did not disappoint, dressed to the nines each day and with her hair and makeup perfectly done. She entered a not guilty plea and stuck to her story that Alwyn Smith had been suicidal over his many failures in life and had killed himself by swallowing regular amounts of ant poison.

Unfortunately for Lee, her attempted recruitment of Margrieta Minaar would prove her undoing. If she was indeed innocent, the prosecutor argued, why had she felt the need to concoct a cover story? Why had she tried to enlist someone to lie on her behalf? Lee's defense attorney responded to these questions by attacking Minaar's credibility, but the damage was already done. The jury pronounced Maria Lee guilty. Asked if she had anything to say before sentence was passed, Lee said simply, "Yes. I repeat that I am not guilty." The judge then donned the black cap and sentenced her to death.

Maria Helena Lee was hanged at Pretoria Central Prison on the morning of Saturday, September, 18, 1948. She protested her innocence right to the very end.

Stella Nickell

It started with a panicked phone call to emergency services in Auburn, Washington, on the late afternoon of June 5, 1986. The caller was a woman named Stella Nickell who reported that her husband, Bruce, had collapsed shortly after swallowing two Excedrin capsules. When emergency personnel arrived at the scene, they found 52-year-old Bruce Nickell lying unconscious and barely breathing, on the floor of the single-wide trailer he shared with his wife. A helicopter was summoned and air-lifted Nickell to Harborview Hospital in Seattle. Sadly, he didn't make it, dying shortly after arrival at the facility. His death was attributed to emphysema.

Six days later, at around 6:40 a.m. on the morning of June 11, 15-year-old Hayley Snow walked to her mother's bedroom. Sue Snow was a bank manager and a stickler for punctuality but, on this morning, she was late coming down for breakfast, and her daughter was worried about her. "Mom?" Hayley called from outside the bedroom door. No answer. "Mom?" she repeated, again getting no reply. All she could hear from within was the sound of running water.

Concerned now, Hayley twisted the handle and entered. The room was empty, but the sound of the water directed her to the bathroom, and it was there that she found her mother. Sue Snow was sprawled unconscious on the floor, a hand clutching at her chest, her breathing labored. Hayley ran immediately to call 911. Paramedics, who arrived soon after, found the 40-year-old barely alive. Like Bruce Nickell, she was rushed to Harborview Hospital and, like him, she died soon after arrival, having never regained consciousness.

Doctors initially suspected that Sue Snow had died of an aneurysm in the brain, but there was one problem with that diagnosis – no evidence of internal bleeding. They then suggested a drug overdose, but Hayley insisted her mother didn't drink or smoke, let alone take drugs. An autopsy was then ordered and delivered a surprise. As soon as the first incision was made, pathologists detected the strong smell of almonds. This is a telltale indicator of cyanide poisoning, and when further tests were run, lethal doses of the toxin were found in Susan Snow's body.

But how had she ingested the poison? The evidence suggested that it may have been via the bottle of Excedrin capsules that had been found standing open on her bathroom counter. Samples of the pills were rushed to the Food and Drug Administration and soon delivered the expected result. The capsules contained cyanide.

The discovery of a tainted commercial painkiller sparked panic among Washington state officials. It brought to mind the case in Chicago four years earlier where someone had placed poisoned Tylenol capsules on supermarket shelves. Seven people had died in that case, and the perpetrator had never been caught.

Desperate to avoid a similar disaster, the authorities contacted the makers of Excedrin, the drug manufacturer Bristol-Myers. They, in turn, issued a nationwide alert and ordered the immediate removal of 30 million bottles of Excedrin, worth more than $100 million, from supermarket shelves. They also offered a reward of $100,000 for information leading to the arrest of the perpetrator. That amount soon swelled to $400,000 as other drug companies contributed to the reward fund.

Aside from the emergency measures put in place to remove Excedrin from the supermarket shelves, there was an investigation to be conducted, a perpetrator to be caught. Legislation enacted since the infamous Tylenol case had made product tampering a federal offense, and so the matter fell under the jurisdiction of the FBI. Sixty agents were assigned and descended on the Auburn area en masse. The initial theory was that the killer was either politically motivated or perhaps a disgruntled employee of Bristol-Myers. That theory would change on June 17. That was the day that Stella Nickell telephoned the police and reported that her husband, Bruce, had also died after taking Excedrin capsules.

Bruce Nickell's death had, of course, been attributed to emphysema. It would most likely never have come to the attention of the police but for the call made by his widow. According to Stella, the bottle of Excedrin that she had in her home had the same lot number as the one that had been in Susan Snow's possession, that number having been broadly published in the media. This made it a matter of interest for the Bureau. When agents arrived at the Nickell home, Stella handed over two bottles of Excedrin, both of which were found to contain cyanide-laced capsules. Bruce Nickell's bloodwork was then re-examined and his death certificate amended. He, too, had been poisoned.

All in all, five bottles of cyanide-laced capsules would be found – one at the Snow residence, two in the Nickell home, and two more on supermarket shelves in the Auburn/Kent area. The poison found in each of these capsules was flecked with small green crystals, determined to come from an algae killer used in home aquariums. This suggested that the killer probably owned a fish tank and had used the same bowl to crush both the algaecide and the arsenic used in the capsules.

But what investigators found truly incredible was that Stella Nickell had purchased two of the tainted packages. A total of 15,000 bottles of Excedrin had been pulled from retail outlets in South King County. Of these, only five had been tampered with. What were the chances that two of those five would end up in the possession of one person? It was possible, of course, if that person had bought the bottles at the same time, but Nickell insisted that she had not. According to her, she'd bought the items two weeks apart and at different locations. The odds of this being a coincidence were off the scale.

With investigators now homing in on Stella Nickell as their main suspect, the evidence soon began stacking up. It was noted that Nickell had a fish tank in her home, thus providing a link to the green flecks of algaecide found in the tainted capsules. Then there were the three insurance policies on Bruce Nickell's life, totaling $75,000 in value but swelled to $175,000 by the accidental death benefit. That caused the investigators to wonder. Had Stella Nickell planted poisoned Excedrin tablets and killed a random stranger simply to boost her insurance payout? Had she endangered countless other lives in order to trigger the accidental death benefit? As diabolical as that idea seemed, the evidence appeared to support it.

And yet, on the surface, Stella Nickell made an unlikely killer. The 42-year-old grandmother worked as a security guard at the Seattle-Tacoma airport and was described by neighbors and colleagues as friendly and hard-working. She and Bruce had seemed happy together, and she appeared genuinely dejected over his death.

Scratch a little deeper, though, and a different picture of Stella Nickell emerged. It turned out that Stella had a police record, one that included convictions for check fraud, forgery, and child abuse. She and Bruce had also been in deep financial trouble, with the bank about to foreclose on their trailer. The payout from the insurance policies would have remedied that situation quite nicely, especially with the accidental death benefit triggered. Perhaps that was why Stella had pestered the doctors after Bruce died, phoning them several times to dispute their finding that her husband had died of natural causes.

Stella Nickell was brought in for questioning on November 18, 1986, and was soon caught in a number of lies. Asked to take a polygraph, she tearfully refused, saying that she couldn't face any more questions. She agreed, however, to take the test once she felt up to it. When she did, four days later, she failed.

This was a strong indicator that Stella had killed her husband and that her actions had also caused the death of Susan Snow. But polygraphs are not infallible and, in any case, are not admissible in court. What investigators really needed was a confession. Unfortunately, it was not one that Stella seemed likely to give. Pressed on the issue, she said that she wanted to speak to her lawyer. Then she clammed up.

Six weeks passed, during which the FBI went back to the evidence and to re-interviewing their witnesses. They were looking for the clue that would help them pressure Stella into making a confession, the missing link that would tie the case together. But they were getting nowhere and beginning to despair that their suspect, like the perpetrator of the 1982 Tylenol murders, would go unpunished. Then, out of the blue, came a surprise turn of events. Cindy Hamilton was Stella's daughter from a previous marriage and had been her staunchest supporter over the course of the investigation. But after the failed polygraph, Cindy had begun to have second thoughts about her mother's innocence. Now she was ready to talk.

According to Cindy, her mother was certainly capable of murder. She had spoken often of killing Bruce and had even once discussed hiring a hitman. Asked about a possible motive, Cindy offered a shocking one. She said that Stella had grown tired of her marriage. She and Bruce had once had an active social life and had spent most nights drinking in local bars. But Bruce had recently undergone treatment for alcoholism and had been on the wagon ever since. These days, he preferred to stay at home, watching TV and messing around with his CB radio. Stella complained often that he had become a bore.

Cindy also provided one other interesting snippet of information. She said that her mother had recently been bringing home books from the local library, books on toxic plants and other poisons. This was easy to verify. Under subpoena, the Auburn Public Library revealed that Stella had indeed checked out books on poisons, including titles like "Deadly Harvest" and "Human Poisoning from Native Plants." Her fingerprints were also found all over the encyclopedias available at the library, concentrated on the pages about cyanide. With motive, means, and opportunity now established, a warrant was issued for Stella Nickell's arrest.

Nickell would be tried in federal court during early 1988. The charges brought against her were not for murder but for product tampering, a serious offence that had been elevated to federal status since the Tylenol poisoning case. Cindy Hamilton was the key prosecution witness, even if many considered her testimony tainted. Hamilton had since pocketed $250,000 in reward money. There were some who speculated that she'd initially been in on the murder plot but had decided to betray her mother once the reward was offered.

Those speculations notwithstanding, the evidence was deemed sufficient to convict Stella Nickell. Describing her crimes as "exceptionally callous and cruel," Judge William Dwyer sentenced Nickell to 99 years in prison, with no parole for at least 30 years. Now in her 70s, Nickell remains behind bars. She continues to proclaim her innocence, insisting that her daughter lied to investigators in order to claim the reward.

Elizabeth Van Valkenburgh

Elizabeth van Valkenburgh was born in Bennington, Vermont, in July 1799. We know very little about her childhood other than what she would later record in her confession – that her parents both died when she was five years old, that she was taken in by a family in Cambridge, New York, and that she received very little education or religious guidance. We know also that she was married for the first time at age 20 and that she lived with her husband in Pennsylvania and later in Johnstown, New York. The marriage was not a happy one, with her husband fond of the bottle and frequently to be found in the local taverns. Nonetheless, it endured until September 1833, when Elizabeth's husband died, apparently of dyspepsia and exposure.

With four children to feed and no means of supporting them, Elizabeth was left with little option but to marry again. This she did within six months of her first husband's death, accepting the proposal of one John Van Valkenburgh and exchanging vows with him in March 1834. The couple would later add two more children to their burgeoning brood.

But Van Valkenburgh turned out to be just another version of Elizabeth's first husband, a hard-drinking hell raiser who frequently abused her and her children when he was under the influence. He also exerted absolute control over Elizabeth. When her two oldest sons, by now grown and settled out west, urged Elizabeth to join them, John stoutly refused to countenance the idea. He also warned her to not even think about deserting him, saying that he'd hunt her down if she tried. Desperate and desperately unhappy, Elizabeth started to look

around for another way out of her predicament. She found it in the
rodents that plagued the rented house in which they were living.

The most common way to get rid of rats in those days was to feed
them arsenic. As such, the poison was freely available and could be
purchased over the counter at any pharmacy. In the fall of 1844,
Elizabeth send a local boy to procure a quantity of the poison for her,
some of which she fed to the rodent population and some of which she
held back for the purpose of poisoning her husband. John was at that
time on one of his frequent binges, at one time staying away from the
family home for eight days. During his absence, Elizabeth tried mixing
some of the poison into a cup of rum and noticed that a powdery white
scum formed on the surface of the liquid. In his state of near
permanent inebriation, John Van Valkenburgh would most likely not
have noticed, but Elizabeth wasn't taking any chances. She mixed the
poison into an urn of boiling water, then stored the water in a bottle
while discarding the residue that settled on the bottom. This would
provide the means of her husband's death.

When John Van Valkenburgh eventually returned from his latest
bender, he was surprised to find his normally quarrelsome wife in an
accommodating mood. Elizabeth asked no questions about his
whereabouts over the previous week and made none of her usual
accusations of infidelity. Instead she prepared a meal for him and then
made him a mug of tea, even adding a dollop of rum to the mix. No
sooner had her husband consumed this than he was violently ill and
afflicted with stomach cramps so severe that he was left writhing on
the floor in agony.

A doctor was called, of course, but Van Valkenburgh would never fully recover. Each time he appeared to be making some progress towards regaining his health, he'd suddenly be struck down by a fresh bout of vomiting, diarrhea, and stomach cramps. When he died, on March 16, 1845, it was almost a mercy.

But Elizabeth had badly miscalculated in her choice of murder weapon. Dr. James Burdick, who had attended her husband, suspected that he'd been poisoned and passed on his suspicions to the authorities. Soon rumors were circulating around the neighborhood that Elizabeth was to be arrested and charged with murder. Informed of this by a sympathetic neighbor, she attempted to flee, taking shelter in a barn near Kingsboro. It was at this location that she was taken into custody, suffering a fall and a broken leg in the process.

Elizabeth Van Valkenburgh was now in a perilous position. Justice moved swiftly in those days, and it did not rest heavily on compassion. Moreover, the evidence was firmly against her, leaving her with little option but to confess her crime and to throw herself on the mercy of the court, such as it was. At trial, she testified that her husband was a drunkard and a scoundrel who "misused" her and the children and frequently left them without money to buy even a crust of bread. She had killed him out of desperation, she said, but now felt remorse for his suffering. "If the deed could have been recalled, I would have done it with all my heart," she told the court. It was a plea that fell on deaf ears. Found guilty of willful murder, she was sentenced to death by hanging, the execution scheduled for January 24, 1846.

In the aftermath of the trial, there was widespread support for the convicted murderess. Governor Silas Wright soon found himself inundated with clemency petitions, including one signed by ten of the twelve jurors who had found Elizabeth guilty of murder. The governor, however, was unmoved by these pleas, saying that he could find no basis in law for calling off the execution.

And with that, Elizabeth was condemned to her fate. To her credit, she appeared to accept it stoically, conceding that she was guilty and that she had received a fair trial. She also had one more confession to make. In the run up to her execution, she admitted that she had also poisoned her first husband by dosing his rum with arsenic. "I always had a very ungovernable temper," she said, "and was so provoked by his going to Mr. Terrill's bar where he had determined to go, and I had threatened that if he did go, he should never go to another bar, and as he did go notwithstanding this, I put in the arsenic as I have said." She ended this second confession by condemning the evils of "rum drinking and rum selling."

Elizabeth Van Valkenburgh died on the gallows at Fulton County Jail on January 24, 1846. Her execution was unique in that she was unable to stand, due to her injured leg and her obesity. Instead, she was seated in a rocking chair and was rocking calmly back and forth when the trap was sprung, sending her to her death.

Jill Coit

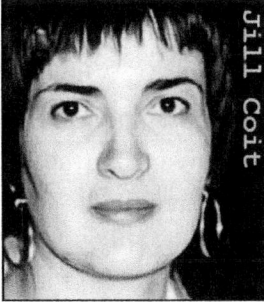

The case of Jill Coit must be one of the most convoluted in the annals of American crime. Coit was a bigamist, a philanderer, a con artist, a teller of tall tales. She was also a murderer and quite possibly a serial killer.

Jill Lonita Billiot was born in Louisiana on June 11, 1943. Her father was a tugboat captain, and Jill had a happy childhood, exploring the bayous and canals around New Orleans. She was a pretty girl, dark-haired and brown-eyed. She was also clever, doing well at school. It was perhaps for that reason that her mother sent her to live with her maternal grandparents in North Manchester, Indiana, when she was in her sophomore year of high school. Juanita Billiot wanted her daughter to attend college after graduation, and there were just too many distractions for her in New Orleans.

However, the diversions would prove just as plentiful in Indiana. Jill fit in easily at school and was soon one of the popular kids. The boys, especially, paid attention, and one of them, Larry Eugene Ihnen, was quite smitten. Fortunately for him, Jill returned his feelings. In July 1961, the two of them dropped out of school, eloped, and were married. Larry was just 18 years old at the time; Jill was seventeen.

But it did not take long for the flush of teen romance to fade. Within nine months, Larry had moved out and returned to his parental home. Just shy of what would have been the couple's first anniversary, the divorce was granted on grounds of cruel and inhumane treatment. Interestingly, the decree noted that Larry was the injured party.

Her first marriage now dissolved, Jill found work at a canning factory but soon realized that drudgery and grime was not for her. What she needed was a meal ticket, and she had more chance of finding one in her home state. Returning south, she completed her high school diploma and then enrolled at Northwestern State University of Louisiana in Natchitoches. It was there that she met husband number two, Steven Moore. Like Larry Ihnen before him, Moore would soon realize that Jill was high maintenance. Not even the arrival of a baby boy, Steven Seth Moore, in March 1965, could hold the marriage together. Within a year, Jill had moved out and was casting around again. This time she had set the bar higher. Her third husband would have to be someone with money.

Enter into the picture one William Clark Coit Jr. Coit wasn't exactly a millionaire, but he made a good living as a gas pipeline engineer and had a sizeable chunk of cash stashed away. At 35, he was older than the twice-married Jill, but that did not stand in the way of romance. Neither did the fact that Jill was still married to Steven Moore. She soon moved into Coit's apartment in the French Quarter of New Orleans. Then she secretly began divorce proceedings. Those proceedings had not yet been finalized when she tied the knot with Clark Coit in January 1966.

Just nine months into her marriage to Coit, Jill delivered a second son, who the couple named William Clark Coit III. Coit also adopted Jill's son by Steven Moore, who she renamed Johnathan Seth Coit. By now, the family had moved to Orange, Texas, where Jill lived a comfortable life as a stay-at-home mom. No luxury was denied her, but her husband was often away, and Jill was not the kind of woman to tolerate boredom. She filled up the time with a string of affairs.

Clark Coit might well have remained oblivious to these indiscretions. But Jill seems to have been the kind of woman who enjoyed inflicting hurt. She openly boasted of her affairs, flaunting them to her husband. Coit, who genuinely loved her, was destroyed. In 1972, heartbroken and humiliated, he filed for divorce. He also took the extraordinary step of withdrawing a sizeable chunk of his fortune from his bank account, telling friends that this was to keep it out of Jill's grasp. "She only married me for my money," he explained woefully. That was on March 8, 1972. Three weeks later, Clark Coit would be dead.

It was Jill who found Clark's body, shot to death, on March 29, 1972. Questioned by the police, she appeared distraught, explaining that, pending divorce aside, she still loved Clark. The investigators didn't believe her. In fact, they were certain that it was she who had fired the fatal bullets. However, by the time they had enough evidence to bring the matter before a grand jury, Jill had fled. Also gone was the money that Clark Coit had withdrawn from his bank account.

Tracking the fugitive was not a difficult matter. She had fled back to her native Louisiana. But Jill was not about to submit to extradition without a fight. She had lawyered up, paying her attorney, Louis DiRosa, with the money she'd stolen from her dead husband. She had also checked herself into a mental facility, citing "acute emotional distress." That put her out of reach of the Texas authorities, and they soon gave up the fight. Over the protests of Clark Coit's family, Jill inherited the balance of his estate.

We next catch up with Jill Coit in August of 1973 in California. There, she somehow wormed her way into the affections of Bruce Johansen, a wealthy retiree in his 90s. There is no indication that this was a romantic involvement. Instead, Coit convinced the old man to "adopt" her. Within a year of doing so, he was dead, and Coit walked away with another handsome inheritance. Although Johansen's death was ultimately put down to natural causes, questions remain over Coit's possible involvement.

The next man to march Jill Coit down the aisle was a U.S. Marine Corps major named Donald Charles Brodie. Unfortunately for Jill, Major Brodie ran a tight ship and kept a firm hand on the purse strings, giving Jill just enough to run the household. This soon became a sticking point in their marriage. Within a year, both parties were retaining lawyers to dissolve the union. But Jill was not going to let go without squeezing as much as she could out of Major Brodie. In October 1974, she informed her husband that she had given birth to a son, who she had named Thadeus John Brodie. He was going to have to cough up for child support. When Brodie insisted on seeing the infant, she produced a newborn for his inspection.

Brodie, though, was not convinced. He asked his lawyers to investigate. When they could find no record of the birth, they hired a P.I. to look into the matter. It soon transpired that Jill had paid a destitute young couple to "borrow" their baby for a few hours. The con had failed. It would not be the last time that Jill played it.

Back in New Orleans after the failure of her latest matrimonial excursion, Jill hooked up with an old ally. Only, this time, her relations with attorney Louis A. DiRosa were of a more personal nature. DiRosa had represented her during her fight against extradition to Texas. Now he was to become her fifth husband. The couple tied the knot in October 1976, but the marriage was volatile, and Jill walked out after barely a year. In March 1978, while still legally married to DiRosa, she exchanged vows with Indiana auctioneer Eldon Duane Metzger. Six months later, she traveled to Haiti to obtain a divorce from Metzger. This jurisdiction was probably chosen to cover up the fact that she and Metzer had never been legally married in the first place. There was money to be squeezed out of a divorce.

Freed from her latest domestic entanglement, Jill hooked up again with DiRosa. Their on-again-off-again relationship endured until 1985 when they were finally divorced, legally this time. By the time the ink dried on the documents, Jill was already two years into her sixth marriage.

The latest man to be reeled in by the serial bigamist was Carl Steely, a teacher at the exclusive Culver Academy in Culver, Indiana. This union would, surprisingly, last for nine years, although it was never actually legal and was far from happy. Jill continued to sleep around and continued to retain her former husband, Louis DiRosa, as legal counsel. In 1990, Carl and Jill vacationed in Steamboat Springs, Colorado, and decided that it would be a good place to retire. The couple decided to buy a bed and breakfast in the town. When the vacation was over, Jill stayed behind to run the place while Carl returned to Culver to finish his last term as a teacher. He returned in the summer to carry out renovations on the place.

But Carl, like so many of Jill's spouses in the past, had been duped. Jill had brought in her old friend DiRosa to oversee the purchase of the B&B, and the lawyer had conveniently left Carl's name off the deed, substituting it with the name of Seth Coit, Jill's eldest son. Carl would only discover the deception when it was too late. He'd later claim that there had been two periods during the marriage when he had suspected that his wife was trying to poison him. He felt fortunate to have escaped the marriage alive. The next man in Jill's life would not be so lucky.

Also living in Steamboat Springs during the time that Jill Coit called it home, was a lifelong bachelor named Gerry Boggs. A graduate of the University of Colorado, Boggs owned a profitable hardware store and was well off. He was an outdoor type, a Vietnam veteran who enjoyed scuba diving, photography and flying. It wasn't long before Jill had fixed her predatory gaze on him. In April 1991, while still ostensibly married to Carl Steely, she accepted his proposal of marriage.

Soon after the couple tied the knot, Jill announced that she was pregnant. This was impossible since she'd had a hysterectomy a few years earlier but Gerry had no way of knowing that. He was ecstatic at the prospect of becoming a father and threw himself into the task of decorating a nursery for the baby. He also accompanied Jill on shopping trips to buy baby clothes and accessories. Then, as the joyous date got closer, Jill announced that she was returning to Louisiana to have the baby. She wanted her child to be born in her home state.

Gerry did not object to the idea, even if business commitments meant that he would have to stay behind. Soon after, Jill departed, only to return weeks later with a tragic tale to tell. She had given birth to a baby girl, she said, but the child had died soon after.

It is difficult to understand what Jill hoped to achieve with this ruse. If it was attention and sympathy, she succeeded admirably. Everyone in town gathered around with messages of support and condolences. Everyone, that is, except Gerry Boggs. Boggs had begun to suspect during the latter part of the "pregnancy" that it was all a scam. Now he did a bit of digging and unearthed some startling facts about his new wife. He learned, for example, that she was still married to someone else and that he was her eighth husband. Armed with this information, Boggs filed for an annulment, which was granted in December 1991.

With her duplicity now uncovered, Jill was persona non grata in Steamboat Springs. In February 1992, she showed up in Las Vegas, Nevada, where she seduced and married Roy Carroll, a retired U.S. Navy Petty Officer. The happy couple then departed for Carroll's hometown of Houston, Texas, where they settled down to married life. But, as always with Jill, marital bliss was short-lived. By the end of the year, she had walked out on her husband and was living with a telephone repairman named Michael Backus. The two had, in fact, started an affair back in Steamboat Springs, while Jill was still with Gerry Boggs and pretending that she was expecting his child.

Boggs, meanwhile, had been getting on with his life. He had been genuinely in love with Jill, and the failure of their relationship had hurt him deeply. He was, however, a pragmatist, who took his knocks and kept going. He was also a diligent man and a creature of habit. You could set your clock by Gerry's routine. He ate breakfast at his favorite diner every morning, always ordering the same menu item. And he always, always, opened his hardware store by 10 a.m.

On the morning of October 22, however, the store sat locked and shuttered. When word of this reached Gerry's brother, Doug, he knew right away that something was wrong. Gerry never missed work. Doug, therefore, got into his car and raced over to his brother's house. There he walked in on a terrible scene. Gerry lay dead on the floor in a pool of blood, several bullet holes perforating his body. It appeared that he had also suffered a severe beating. An autopsy would later determine that he had been incapacitated with a Taser and that his killer had then bludgeoned him with a shovel before ending his life with a .22 caliber weapon.

It did not take long before investigators had a suspect in their sights. It was common knowledge in Steamboat Springs that Gerry Boggs and his wife had been involved in an acrimonious dispute over the ownership of the B&B. Boggs had put a substantial amount of money into renovating the property and was claiming part ownership. Jill had responded by launching a civil suit against him. In the run up to the trial, Boggs had collected a number of threatening messages that Jill had left on his answering machine. He had played these to his brother and had told him that he intended using them as evidence. The answering machine was the only item missing from the Boggs residence. The only person who had a motive for removing it was Jill. At the time, she was living with Michael Backus, just an hour's drive from the crime scene.

Brought in for questioning, Jill and Backus quickly offered up an alibi. They claimed that they had been camping in Poudre Canyon, west of Fort Collins, at the time of the murder. Jill also suggested an alternative suspect. She said that Gerry had been a closet homosexual and recommended that they track down his gay lover. To the police, many of whom had known Gerry Boggs, it was an outrageous claim that didn't warrant any investigative time. They did, however, have to check out the couple's alibi. While they were doing so, the suspects slipped across the border to Mexico, thus avoiding arrest. It appeared that Jill had gotten away with murder, just as she had in the case of Clark Coit.

The flight from justice would, however, be a short one. Jill had been forced to flee with very little money, and it soon ran out. In December 1993, she and Michael Backus crossed back into the US and headed for Colorado. In the interim, she had given her son Seth power of attorney over the B&B and told him to start looking for a buyer. The proceeds of the sale would allow her to continue living as a fugitive in Mexico. Fortunately, her plans had been leaked to the police (perhaps by Seth, although this has never been confirmed). Shortly after they reached Colorado, the fugitives were arrested.

By now, the police had built up a substantial case against the pair. They had learned, for example, that Jill had approached several people with offers of cash for carrying out a hit on Gerry Boggs. She had told them that she wanted him dead because he had been sexually molesting her daughter (she did not have a daughter, only two sons). Backus had made similar offers, to a friend and to a co-worker, saying that he wanted to get rid of Gerry because he had forced Jill into having sex with other men while he watched.

The biggest break in the case, however, came when Seth Coit decided to speak up against his mother. Seth had long suspected that Jill had killed his adoptive father, Clark Coit; he knew for certain that she was involved in the death of Gerry Boggs. He told investigators that his mother had phoned him on the night that Gerry was killed. "It's over," she had told him. "It was messy."

Jill Coit and Michael Backus were formally indicted for murder on December 23, 1993. With bond set at $5 million each, they would remain behind bars until their trial in 1995. Convicted of first-degree murder and conspiracy to commit murder, they were both sentenced to life in prison without the possibility of parole.

Life in prison has not been without incident for the much-married Jill Coit. In December 1998, she recruited a friend to run a personal ad for her. "Want U.S. Citizenship?" it read. "Marry an inmate." It seems that, even behind bars, she was still trying to lure men into her web of deceit. Unfortunately for her, the U.S. Department of Naturalization and Immigration shut down her ad before there were any takers.

In 2002 and again in 2006, Coit filed suit against the Colorado Department of Corrections claiming sexual and physical assault. The claims were found to be frivolous but nonetheless resulted in her being moved to an out-of-state facility. Her current whereabouts are believed to be a medium-security prison in Nebraska.

Maggie Young

It was a crime that shocked the nation. On June 20, 2001, a 35-year-old Houston housewife name Andrea Yates murdered her five children, aged six months to seven years. Yates had taken the children one by one to the bathroom, placed them in a tubful of water and systematically drowned them. Later, the deeply religious Yates would claim that her children were not developing righteously and that she'd murdered them in order to save their souls from the "fires of hell." She was initially sentenced to life in prison, although she was later declared not guilty by reason of insanity and sent to a mental institution. The case continues to divide opinion to this day. Astonishingly, it is not the first of its kind. In 1965, in Hawaii, a woman named Maggie Young committed a near identical mass slaughter.

Maggie Young was the wife of an Air Force pilot, Captain James Young, who was based at Hickam Air Force Base in Pearl Harbor, Hawaii. Captain Young was Maggie's second husband, and she already had two adult daughters from a previous marriage when she tied the knot with the flyer. Their union would subsequently be blessed with five children: James Jr., Janice, Judith, Jeanette, and Jessica. When our story takes place, James Jr. was eight years old. Jessica, the youngest, was just eight months.

As in the case of Andrea Yates, no one knows the precise trigger that drove Maggie Young to commit such an outrageous atrocity. Like Yates, she was a deeply religious woman, her belief bordering on mania; like Yates, she'd suffered from severe postpartum depression after the birth of her youngest. Where Yates had feared for the immortal souls of her offspring, Young had questioned her own abilities as a mother. She worried that she might be unfit to raise her children. Like Andrea Yates, she'd spent time in a mental hospital in the run up to the killings but had been released, with tragic results.

And yet, the danger signs were there for all to see. Young had been deeply depressed in the months after Jessica's birth. She was unhappy and expressed feelings of inadequacy. She was constantly tired, sometimes failing to rise in the morning, at other times crawling into bed fully clothed in the middle of the day, leaving her children unfed and uncared for. James Young would come home from work to find the children in dirty diapers, crying and hungry. He'd then have to change them, feed them, give them their baths and get them ready for bed. Through all of this, Maggie didn't even bother to get up. Eventually, the situation got so bad that James had to call on his wife's two adult daughters to help out.

But if James Young was annoyed about his wife's uncaring behavior, he'd soon have reason to be genuinely concerned. Soon Maggie would begin suffering delusions and hallucinations. In one particular incident, she went missing for three hours before returning in the middle of the night. Asked where she had been, she said that she had attended church. She then dismayed her husband by telling him that God had spoken to her as she prayed. He'd told her that he (James) was actually Jesus and that his grandmother had been the Blessed Virgin. That was not the only bizarre occurrence. A few days later, James was about to leave for work when his wife appeared out of nowhere and started hitting him with a broomstick. "Don't open the door," she hissed. "They are out there. They've come to kill me." It was after this incident that James decided to have her committed.

But getting psychiatric help for the quite obviously ailing Maggie
would prove more difficult than James had expected. Administrators at
Tripler Army Medical Center told him that he could not commit
Maggie to the hospital involuntarily, that she would have to consent to
entering the facility. This, Maggie refused to do. Eventually, James
had to call on the help of their priest to convince her that it was "God's
will."

Maggie Young would remain in the hospital for six weeks, making no
discernible progress. Eventually, James was called to a conference
with her doctors and advised to take her home, which they felt was the
best environment for her recovery. And for a while, it seemed that they
were right. Maggie wasn't back to her old self, but at least she wasn't
talking about conversations with God or assassins coming to kill her.
There was certainly no inkling that she was dangerous or might harm
the children.

On November 22, 1965, Captain James Young was sent on a flying
mission out of Hickam Air Force Base. Maggie was at home with the
four girls, while James Jr. was packed off to attend classes at Alvah
Scott Elementary School, just a stone's throw away from the Young
residence on Nalopaka Place. This, however, was no ordinary day.
James Jr. was barely out of the door when Maggie walked to the
bathroom and ran a tubful of water. She then called out to five-year-
old Janice, grabbing the child as she entered the room, forcing her into
the tub and holding her head under water until she stopped thrashing.
She then carried the lifeless body to the girl's bedroom, stripped it
naked and laid it out on one of the twin beds.

This contrived, callous process was repeated again with Judith, with Jeanette, even with 8-month-old Jessica. Eventually, with her four daughters lying lifeless on the bed, Maggie Young walked to Alvah Scott Elementary and pulled her son out of school. It was now 9:30 a.m. James Jr. was walked home by his mother, taken to the bathroom and overpowered. His naked, drowned body was laid out in the same room as his sisters but on a separate bed. Maggie Young then calmly phoned the police and told them what she had done. Later, under interrogation, she expressed no remorse for her actions. She said that she'd killed her children in order to remove them from a cruel world. She'd sent them to a better place, to be with God.

Despite admitting to causing the deaths of all five children, Young was charged only with the murder of her son, James Jr. And it was never likely that she would be convicted on that charge. Examined by a panel of court-appointed psychiatrists, she was declared to have been acting under a "diseased and deranged condition" and, therefore, unfit to stand trial. Instead, she was sent to the Hawaii State Hospital in Kaneohe. There, doctors soon reported that she was responding well to treatment and beginning to understand the enormity of what she'd done. That realization, however, came at a cost. Six months into her incarceration, Maggie Young escaped from her ward and went wandering the hospital grounds. She was found hours later in a shed, hanging by the neck from a makeshift noose.

For James Young, it was another tragedy, piled upon the one he was already suffering. James had not yet begun to come to terms with the loss of his children, although he had begun to accept that mental illness had driven his wife to commit the atrocity. He would later move to California and eventually remarry, although he would father no more children. In 2001, he was surprised to receive a call from Andrea Yates's husband Russell, reaching out in an effort to make sense of the dreadful tragedy that had befallen him. The two men spoke for several hours, with Young providing advice and solace. Who better than he to understand what Russell Yates was going through.

Rekha Kumari-Baker

Divorce can be a messy business. Take the case of David and Rekha Kumari-Baker, for example. David was a successful businessman from Stretham, in Cambridgeshire, England. Rekha was an Indian-born beauty. The couple had met in the '90s and married after a whirlwind romance. Theirs seemed a match made in heaven, but after a decade together, the strain was showing. Not even the two daughters they'd raised could paper over the cracks. Finally, in 2003, they agreed that it was over and that their lives would be better spent apart. The divorce was uncontested with Rekha gaining custody of the girls, Davina, 12, and Jasmine, 9. David was granted full visitation rights. They had parted on more or less civil terms. When Rekha started dating a man named Jeff Powell, David was happy for her. So far, so good.

But then things had started to go seriously wrong in Rekha's life. First, David started seeing someone new, a woman named Kadi Kone who Rekha soon came to despise. Before David started dating Kadi, Rekha had told anyone who would listen that she was over him and was deeply in love with Jeff Powell. But now, all of that changed. She seemed to resent David's happiness and was particularly opposed to her daughters spending time with Kadi. Perhaps as a result of that bitterness, she and older daughter Davina started clashing, a situation that got so bad that Davina eventually moved out and went to live with her father. That caused Rekha, a volatile woman at the best of times, to suffer from depression. Her mood swings became pronounced and unpredictable, and that inevitably put a strain on her relationship with Jeff. By 2007, Jeff had reached the end of his tether and told her that it was over. No amount of begging could get him to change his mind. Finally, to add to her burgeoning catalog of woes, Rekha lost her waitressing job.

Rekha's life, it seemed, was disintegrating before her eyes. Worse still, there was David, who appeared to be blissfully contented in his new relationship. That did not sit well with Rekha, who could not bear to see her ex happy while she was suffering. As she sat at home, jobless, alone and bitter, she started plotting revenge against David. What would hurt him most? What would be the deepest cut, the one from which he'd never recover? From this tainted ground, a plan began to sprout, a dreadful, selfish plan that involved the destruction of two innocent young lives.

On Tuesday, June 14, 2007, Rekha contacted her daughter Davina, now 16, and asked if she wanted to join her and Jasmine for a shopping trip. Davina's relationship with her mother was not in the best place at that time, so she wavered at first. But Rekha's enthusiasm for the idea soon won her over. Which teenaged girl can resist the lure of a shopping spree? Besides, maybe this was a chance to build bridges. Jasmine would be there, too. Perhaps this would be the mother/daughter bonding session that they all needed.

As it turned out, that was precisely the case. Rekha and her daughters enjoyed a fun day out, traveling to the Lakeside Mall, 50 miles away in Essex. They arrived home late in the evening, tired but exhilarated. Given the hour, Rekha suggested that Davina stay over, and Davina was happy to do so. After checking with her father, she carried her purchases upstairs and settled into her old room. Later that night, she sent Rekha a text that would have warmed any mother's heart. "Thanks. I really enjoyed myself. I love you with all my heart and always will." It was the last communication that would ever pass between them.

At around 2:30 the following morning, while the rest of the household was asleep, Rekha Kumari-Baker roused herself, left her bedroom, and headed downstairs to the kitchen. There she retrieved two long-bladed knives, purchased just two days earlier from an ASDA supermarket. These she carried upstairs, into the room occupied by her older daughter, Davina. The teen was fast asleep when her mother fell on her, launching a frenzied attack, stabbing and slashing. Davina tried to fight back, but she was at a disadvantage, caught by surprise, trapped by the blankets, unable to resist the ferocity of the onslaught. Eventually, she lay still and resisted no more, a bloody mess of ruptured organs, severed veins, and torn tissue.

Then, without a second thought, Rekha left the room and headed down the hall to where 13-year-old Jasmine lay asleep. She must have been quite a sight in her blood-drenched nightdress, wild-eyed and with the blade in her hand, dripping gore. Fortunately, it was a sight that Jasmine never got to see. The little girl was knifed to death while she slept. The coroner would later determine that she had been stabbed 30 times. Davina had suffered 39 knife wounds. Neither of them had stood a chance.

So what did Rekha Kumari-Baker do next, now that she had so savagely slain her two daughters? Did she attempt suicide? Did she call the police and confess her crime? No, Rekha sat down to write a note, a self-pitying missive in which she bemoaned the failure of her relationship with Jeff Powell.

"I've killed my two daughters," she wrote. "I did not want them to get hurt like I did. Jeff hurt me so much I cannot explain. He found it difficult to compromise at times, but I loved him so much. My kids will not be a burden with anyone anymore." Then, with that off her chest, she went for a drive, later returning to the house to shower and change. Finally, at 6:30 a.m., she phoned a friend, a police constable named Natalie Barford. "I've done something terrible," she said. "I've killed the kids."

Kumari-Baker was arrested that same day. At her trial, held at the Cambridge Crown Court in September 2009, she entered a plea of not guilty to murder but guilty of manslaughter on the grounds of diminished responsibility due to an "abnormality of the mind." Unfortunately for her, she had already been assessed by a team of psychiatrists in the run up to her court appearance. They had found no evidence of mental disorder. If Kumari-Baker was suffering from anything at all, it was a mild form of depression known as Mixed Anxiety Depressive Disorder, which does not require specialist intervention.

What would become evident in the trial testimony is that Kumari-Baker was a narcissistic and volatile individual who cared little for the needs of others. She seemed especially oblivious to the feelings of her daughters and seemed to regard them as possessions. Davina, in particular, had been a target for her caustic and hurtful remarks. On one occasion, she had told the then 14-year-old that she wished she were dead. This was said in front of teachers at the child's school. Those same teachers described Kumari-Baker as a "volatile, excitable, erratic, and sometimes aggressive" individual. Social Services had also been alerted and had been monitoring the family.

But the thing that had most annoyed Rekha was the fact that her ex-husband was building a life without her. That appears to have been the one factor that had pushed her over the edge. In the words of the prosecutor, the murders had been committed in order to punish David Baker, in order to "destroy the happiness in his life." If that truly was her intention, she had succeeded beyond measure.

Jury deliberations in modern trials are often protracted affairs, sometimes going on for days before a verdict is reached. In this case, the jurors debated for merely half-an-hour before returning with a unanimous decision. Rekha Kumari-Baker was guilty of two counts of murder. The sentence of the court was as harsh as they come in the British justice system – life in prison with a minimum tariff of 33 years. Kumari-Baker was 41 years old on the day she started her sentence. She will be 72 by the time she becomes eligible for parole.

Corrine Sykes

It was the O.J. Simpson case of its day, a case that divided observers more or less along racial lines. To the white citizens of Philadelphia, Corrine Sykes was a stone cold killer who had conned her way into the home of a wealthy society matron with the sole purpose of committing robbery and murder. To the African-American populace of North Philly, Corrine was a simple-minded girl, manipulated into participating in the crime by her no-good boyfriend. She probably hadn't killed her employer, but even if she had, her mental deficiency should exclude her from the harshest punishment. The truth, as it usually does, lay somewhere in between.

The year was 1944, and the city of Philadelphia was on a war footing. With hostilities still raging in Europe and the Far East, and American troops now involved in the fray, the wartime economy was booming. And with the majority of eligible males involved in the fighting abroad, it fell to the women to operate the production lines that fed the war effort. It was an era in which there were jobs to be had if you wanted them and were deemed to have the requisite skills.

But not everyone was lucky enough to land a war industry job. A common sight during this era was of young Black girls, mostly from North Philadelphia, gathered on street corners in affluent neighborhoods, hoping to be picked up for a day's domestic work or perhaps even a longer assignment. On a frigid, early December day in 1944, Corrine Sykes was among these hopefuls and had positioned herself on swanky West Oak Lane. Fortune would smile on Corrine this day, as she was picked up by a wealthy society matron named Freda Wodlinger. Even better news for Corrine was that Mrs. Wodlinger was looking for a long-term housemaid. Provided, of course, the prospective employee could provide suitable references.

Corrine Sykes had references all right but they were a lie. In fact, she'd been fired from her previous job (and several others before that) for stealing. Fortunately for Corrine, Mrs. Wodlinger barely appeared to be listening as she rattled off a list of her former employers, none of them true. "Come along," the elderly woman said eventually. "I'm sure you'll be fine." That was how Corrine Sykes ended up working in the Wodlinger household. Her tenure there would be of short duration. And it would end in tragedy.

On December 7, 1944, three days after Corrine started her new job, her employer, Freda Wodlinger, was found dead, brutally stabbed in her own parlor, her death inflicted by a large kitchen knife. Mrs. Wodlinger had not died easily and had put up a ferocious struggle before being overpowered by her killer. Missing from the house were $50 in cash, $2000 in jewelry, and a sable fur wrap. Also missing was the new housemaid, Corrine Sykes.

As news of the savage killing began to filter out to a shocked populace, a search was launched for Corrine, one that was soon resolved when she was found hiding at a friend's house in North Philly. Taken into custody, she immediately incriminated herself by telling conflicting stories, blaming, among others, her boyfriend, James "Jayce" Kelly, a local hoodlum. According to Corrine, Kelly had threatened to kill her and her mother if she didn't steal for him.

But the police weren't interested in hearing about Kelly. What they wanted was a confession. And so they continued to browbeat the mentally-challenged Corrine for hours until she eventually cracked and admitted that she'd killed her employer after she'd been caught stealing. She then signed a written confession to the crime, although it is debatable whether she knew what was in the document since she could neither read nor write. She did, however, lead the police to the murder weapon, which had been hidden under a piano in the Wodlinger residence.

It was as close to a slam dunk case as any prosecutor could ever wish for. And Corrine's court-appointed lawyer made it even more so when he announced to the jury, "We will make no attempt to exculpate Corrine Sykes in this shocking crime." Instead, Raymond Pace Alexander based his defense strategy on proving that Corrine was mentally slow, emotionally unstable, and under the influence of a boyfriend who had put her up to the crime. To this extent, Alexander produced a psychiatrist who told the jury that the defendant was a "constitutional psychopathic inferior." He also entered into evidence an IQ test which Corrine had taken at age 13. She'd scored 63, giving her the mental capacity of a seven-year-old.

But there were other arguments that the defense counsel might have raised had he not been so dead set on declaring his client guilty and relying on the jury to show mercy. He might, for example, have homed in on the fact that Mrs. Wodlinger's savage wounds were unlikely to have been inflicted by someone as slightly built as Corinne. He might also have offered an alternate suspect – Jayce Kelly, for example. Kelly had been the sole beneficiary of the crime since Corrine had handed over all of the loot to him. Later, after hearing of Corrine's arrest, he'd gone immediately to his apartment where he'd burned the fur wrap. He'd then carried $2000 worth of diamond jewelry outside and dropped the items through a sewer grate. Were these the acts of an innocent man?

Kelly would appear as a prosecution witness at the trial and would deny any involvement in the murder, although he did admit to receiving stolen goods. That admission would ultimately earn him five years in jail, but for Corrine the consequences were far worse. She was found guilty of murder and sentenced to die in the electric chair.

There was considerable sympathy for Corrinne Sykes after the sentence was announced, even among those who had previously condemned her. But few expected that the state would actually go through with the execution. There was very little appetite for executing women in Pennsylvania. Governors usually commuted death sentences passed on female prisoners to life in prison. Even before the trial, the Philadelphia Tribune had run a story under the headline: "Death Penalty Unlikely for Maid in Murder Case."

The Corrine Sykes case, however, was the one that broke the rule. Both the state and U.S. Supreme Courts rejected appeals filed by her attorney, and Governor Edward Martin declined to intercede. The case was a perilous one for him politically. Many of his most prominent constituents employed black domestic help, and they were angry and fearful over the Wodlinger murder. A message had to be sent.

And so it was that, on October 14, 1946, Corrine Sykes made the short walk from the condemned cell to the electric chair at the Pennsylvania State Penitentiary. She was just 22 years old on the day that she made that fateful journey, but those who were present said that she did so without the slightest hint of fear. Condemned male inmates usually have their entire heads shaven but in Corinne's case, only a small spot at the back of her head had been cleared to accommodate the electrode. She sat stock still as this was fixed in place and her wrists were strapped to the chair's armrests. Then the black hood was placed over her head and two jolts of electricity were passed through her body. At 12:31 a.m., Corrine Sykes was pronounced dead.

So what are we to make of this controversial case? Was it a case of justice served or justice perverted? Did the right person end up in the electric chair or was Corrine Sykes an innocent victim of the justice system?

There is an idiom oft used by prosecutors when putting a case before a jury – "the facts don't lie." This is a sensible assertion and most likely true. What they fail to mention is that the conclusions drawn from these immutable facts are often flawed. Did Corrine Sykes murder Freda Wodlinger? In all likelihood, yes. The only other suspect was Jayce Kelly, and he had an alibi. Did Corrine Sykes decide on a whim to rob and murder her employer? The answer to that must be an equally resounding, "no." The most likely explanation is that Sykes was caught stealing and committed murder (probably during a struggle) to conceal her crime. There can be little doubt that Kelly, the recipient of the stolen goods, put her up to it. There can also be little doubt that a modern jury would not have sent Corrine Sykes to her death. After all, we do not execute seven-year-olds.

Cora Caro

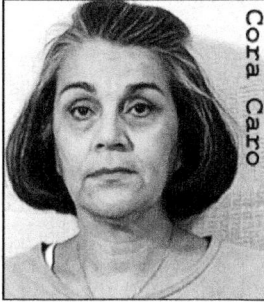

On the face of it, Xavier and Socorro Caro had the perfect marriage, the perfect life. Xavier was a prominent rheumatologist with a booming medical practice in Northridge, California. Socorro (known to all as Cora) was a qualified nurse who had given up her career to run her husband's office. The couple had four sons, Joey, 11, Michael, 8, Christopher, 5, and baby Gabriel, just a few months old. They were deeply religious and active in their church and community. They lived in a million-dollar mansion in picturesque Santa Rosa Valley, California. Aside from her duties at her husband's office, Cora was an excellent cook and a devoted mom who adored her boys.

That was the picture postcard version, the version that the outside world saw. But behind closed doors, the situation was far, far different. Both Xavier and Cora were drinkers and, in Cora's case, the consumption verged on substance abuse. This would often lead to arguments that sometimes spilled over into actual violence, with Cora usually the aggressor. Xavier was often seen sporting cuts and bruises. On one occasion, he even needed hospital treatment for a serious eye injury. After that incident, he suggested to his wife that she start taking anti-depressants. He even wrote her a prescription, but that turned out to be a bad move. Cora was soon popping fistfuls of pills, washing them down with whiskey.

Xavier, meanwhile, had his own vices. He was having an affair with one of his employees, an attractive respiratory therapist. When Cora found out, there was the predictable eruption, followed by a renewed round of domestic confrontations. Then Xavier discovered that his wife had been siphoning off money from his medical practice, embezzling nearly $100,000. Cora claimed that she had given the money to her father, a builder who had done repairs on the couple's home after a recent earthquake but had never been paid. Xavier, however, was furious at his wife's deception. Shortly after the theft came to light, he secretly consulted a divorce lawyer. Cora found out about this when she was going through his pockets and came across a pro-forma schedule of the marital assets. The inevitable row followed with Xavier eventually storming out and Cora finding solace in her booze and pills.

As the 1990s drew to a close, the situation in the Caro household continued to simmer just below boiling point. And a new and terrifying dynamic had been added to the mix. Cora was talking openly about suicide, telling several of her friends that she saw no point in carrying on. During one telephone conversation, she even mentioned that she was holding her husband's gun in her hand and was tempted to put it in her mouth and pull the trigger. That bizarre phone call sent the woman scuttling to Xavier's office where she warned him that Cora was talking crazy and might harm herself. But Xavier laughed it off. He said that his wife was just looking for attention. That would prove to be a gross misreading of the situation.

The night of November 22, 1999, was a typical one in the Caro household. The family had enjoyed an evening meal together and the boys had then gone up to play in their rooms while Xavier and Cora remained downstairs for an after-dinner margarita. It was all very civil, but still the atmosphere was tense, a powder keg waiting to blow. It would only take one small spark, and that arrived in the form of 11-year-old Joey. The little boy was obviously aware that his parents and alcohol were a volatile mix. He had taken it on himself to avert trouble by asking them not to drink too much. Unfortunately, his father took the attempted intervention as impertinence and grounded him on the spot. That set Cora off. She accused Xavier of being too hard on the children. He responded by saying that she was too indulgent with them. It escalated from there into a screaming match. Eventually, Xavier walked out, saying that he was going to the office to catch up on some paperwork.

This was a common avoidance strategy for Xavier. He knew that there was no reasoning with Cora when she was in one of her moods, and so he simply removed himself from the situation, gave her time to cool down, and then snuck back into the house after the family had gone to sleep. But tonight would be different. Tonight Cora wouldn't let it rest. She made several calls to Xavier, accusing him of being uncaring, of failing to grasp the difference between right and wrong. With each of these calls, it was clear that she was becoming steadily more intoxicated. She had continued drinking and popping pills. Her voice had taken on a detached, robotic quality. That alone, should have been a warning to Xavier.

Back at the house, Cora was putting the children to bed. This was a nightly ritual, and she always carried it out, come what may. First she would read a verse from a miniature Bible that each of the boys owned. Then they would pray together before Cora slid the Bible

under the child's pillow and kissed him goodnight. She would turn out
the light on her way out.

But on the night of November 22, Cora paid a second visit to each of
her sons, about an hour later, when she was sure they would be asleep.
This time, she carried in her hand her husband's 9mm pistol. She had
decided that her life was no longer worth living and had resolved to
end it. She had also decided to take her children with her. Whether this
was some warped idea of motherly love or an act of revenge against
her husband, we shall never know.

Five-year-old Christopher was the first to die. Shot at close range
while he slept, he would never have known a thing. Michael, 8, was
killed in similar fashion. But 11-year-old Joey had been awakened by
the gunshots and was sitting up in bed when his mother came through
the door. Still Cora never wavered. Lifting the gun, she fired two
shots, hitting Joey in the head and chest and killing him instantly. His
frantic cry of "Mom!" died with the boom of the pistol. Now only
baby Gabriel remained alive.

Cora's plan had been to kill all four of her sons. But as she crossed the
nursery and stood over the crib, she found that she could not bring
herself to shoot the infant who had, until recently, been suckling at her
breast. Instead she left the room, closing the door behind her. Then she
walked to the hallway and there inserted the barrel of the gun into her
mouth. She wanted her body to be the first thing that Xavier saw when
he entered the house.

In the early hours of November 23, 1999, a Ventura County 911 dispatcher fielded a call from a near-hysterical man. He was screaming that his children were dead, that his wife had shot them and then shot herself. Units were immediately dispatched to the scene and arrived to find a bloodbath. Joey, Michael, and Christopher were all dead, shot to death in their beds. Cora, miraculously was still alive. The bullet had ripped through her upper palate and had lodged in her brain, but it hadn't killed her. She was rushed to a nearby hospital, where emergency surgery would save her life, albeit that she suffered some brain damage and memory loss.

Cora Caro was brought to trial at the Ventura County Superior Court in August 2001. She was charged with three counts of murder and initially entered an insanity plea. However, she later changed her mind and pled "not guilty" instead. Her defense then set about trying to pin the murders on Xavier Caro. Their theory was that Xavier had murdered his sons, then shot his wife in a way that looked like an attempted suicide in an effort to pin the murders on her. The jury was never going to believe that farfetched version of events and, in any case, it was not supported by the forensic evidence. Cora was also unable to provide any insight into the shootings. She claimed (perhaps conveniently) that the self-inflicted bullet wound had wiped out any memory she had of that terrible night.

This was a highly charged trial with the defendant breaking down several times during testimony and, at one point, angrily confronting her husband in the courtroom. "How could you do this to us?" she screamed at Xavier. Then, getting no response, she turned to court officials, "Look at him! He's smirking at me! He's smirking!"

If this outburst was aimed at painting Xavier in a bad light, it failed dismally. All it did was to show the court what a hysterical, unstable individual Cora Caro was. After deliberating for five days, the ten-woman, two-man jury returned a verdict of guilty. On April 5, 2002, Judge Donald Coleman pronounced sentence of death. He described the murders as "willful, premeditated, and committed with malice aforethought." Cora Caro currently awaits execution at San Quentin State Prison.

Shirley Winters

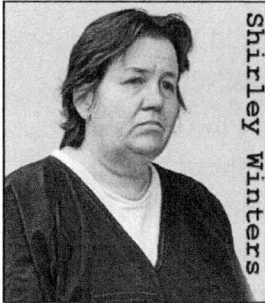

Death, which would become a constant traveling companion to Shirley Winters, visited her for the first time when she was just a child. It happened in 1966, when Shirley was eight years old and a gas leak at the family home, in upstate New York, killed three of her siblings. Her sisters, Joyce, 10, and Lita, aged four, were asphyxiated in their beds. So too was her 11-year-old brother, Peter. By rights, Shirley should have died, too, but she was away that night at her grandmother's house. Joyce had actually been meant to attend the sleepover, but Shirley had nagged until her older sister had relented and allowed her to go in her stead. Thus Joyce died and Shirley lived. She would be plagued by survivor's guilt for the rest of her life. It was a burden that she refused to bear alone.

Who knows the trauma that this tragedy must have inflicted on so young a mind? Shirley did not bear her grief well. She became a difficult child, prone to violent outbursts. This was made worse by the teasing she endured from her classmates, who called her "Squirrelly Shirley." She would respond to these taunts by attacking anyone who was in striking distance, lashing out with fists and nails. Counselling failed to address the problem nor dull her fierce temper as she reached adolescence.

In 1977, at age 18, Shirley married 21-year-old Ronald Winters Jr., settling down with him in the small town of Theresa, New York. She would birth two children, Colleen and John, over the next couple of years. That was when the trouble started. On September 12, 1979, a fire broke out at the Winters residence. Ronald was at work at the time, leaving Shirley home alone with the children. According to Shirley's later report, she'd fallen asleep on the couch and been awakened by the smell of smoke. Somehow, she'd managed to escape the blaze. Her children had not. A subsequent investigation ruled the fire accidental, caused apparently by some kindling that had been left near a wood-burning stove. The police attached no significance to a startling coincidence. On the day prior to the Winters fire, another devastating house fire, in nearby Hermon, New York, had claimed the lives of three children. That blaze had occurred at the home of one of Shirley Winters's friends.

The death of a child can derail even the strongest of marriages, and the Winters's union had been shaky to begin with. Ronald blamed Shirley for the deaths of their children, and the couple soon separated, despite Shirley being pregnant with their third child. Ronald Winters III was born in July 1980, but his young life would be cut even shorter than those of his siblings. On November 21, 1980, paramedics were summoned to Shirley Winters's trailer in Otisco, New York, where they found the baby unresponsive. He was pronounced dead at the scene with the death attributed to Sudden Infant Death Syndrome.

During the early eighties, fire became a recurring theme in Shirley's life. Her trailer appeared to be a magnet for unexplained blazes, with the fire department called out twice in February 1981 alone. Eventually, it was determined that the fires had been deliberately set, and Winters was charged with arson. She was still awaiting trial on that charge when she committed another act of arson resulting in a second arrest. By now reunited with her husband Ronald, she'd face no jail time for any of these charges. Over the next three years, she'd have three more children – Joy, born 1984; Ashley, born 1985; and Clayton born in 1987. She'd also continue her career as a serial arsonist, starting numerous fires including one that broke out at the couple's apartment building in Marcellus, New York, on November 12, 1986. Eventually, it all became too much for Ronald Winters. In 1987, he and Shirley divorced. Thereafter, she moved with her children to Syracuse.

But the change of scenery did nothing to cure the compulsive firebug in Shirley Winters. In 1989, she was arrested on arson charges in Syracuse. While awaiting trial, two small blazes broke out at properties where she was staying while another destroyed a garage at her aunt's home. Then, on November 12, 1989, a basement storage room caught fire at the Winters residence on Willis Avenue in Syracuse. Shirley managed to get out with Ashley and Clayton, but Joy was trapped inside. Fortunately, the little girl was able to escape the flames. Later, she'd tell firefighters that her mother had instructed her to remain inside the house, even as the fire burned around her. Had she not disobeyed that order, she would almost certainly have died.

The Willis Avenue fire did, at least, have one positive outcome. After Shirley was yet again charged with arson, a Family Court judge removed Joy, Ashley, and Clayton from her custody and sent them to live with their father. In doing so, he more than likely saved the children's lives.

Because Shirley Winters's deadly compulsion continued unabated, despite her problems with the law. On April 10, 1990, she set fire to her apartment at 124 Lakeview Avenue; on September 21, she attempted to burn down her aunt's newly rebuilt garage. Unsuccessful in that attempt, she returned two weeks later, this time succeeding in burning the garage and the house with it. Arrested the following day, she responded by attacking a deputy and damaging a patrol car. An additional charge was added when it was found that she had set another fire, at a bowling alley in Camillus, New York. Miraculously, she again avoided a custodial sentence.

Over the next six years, there were at least 18 fires connected to Shirley Winters, although she was never charged with any of them. But her luck was about to run out. On April 27, 1997, there was a serious fire at the home of Winters's mother in Pierrepoint, New York. Arrested for setting the blaze, Winters wasted little time in admitting to it, even telling investigators that she knew that her young nephew was asleep inside when she struck the match. Fortunately, he escaped the burning house. Winters's guilty plea would earn her an 8-year prison term. She was out on parole in 2004, but was soon back inside on a violation, after she was found in possession of a cigarette lighter. She was finally released on June 14, 2005.

And that release would spell doom for another child. On November 28, 2006, Winters was visiting her mother in Pierrepoint. Also visiting at the time was her cousin, Conijean Rivers-Gollinger and her children, including 23-month-old Ryan Rivers. At some point, the

children were left in Winters's care, and during that time, the little boy
was found dead. An autopsy would reveal that he had drowned, most
likely in the bathtub.

Shirley Winters was arrested and charged with murder. In the wake of
that charge, exhumation orders were issued for her children Colleen,
John, and Ronald. The results of the autopsies were stunning. Colleen
and John both had fractures to their skulls, indicating that they'd both
been rendered unconscious and then left to perish in the fire. Young
Ronald had not died of SIDS, as had been thought; he'd been
asphyxiated.

Facing multiple murder charges and with a mass of incriminating
evidence against her, Shirley Winters was left with little option other
than to ask for a plea bargain. A deal was then struck, with prosecutors
forgoing charges in the murders of Colleen and John, in exchange for
guilty pleas relating to the deaths of Ryan Rivers and Ronald Winters
III. Yet the punishment that Winters received hardly fit the crimes. She
was sentenced to 20 years in St. Lawrence County and received an 8-
to-25-year term in Onondaga County. The sentences were to run
concurrently, meaning that Winters may well be free one day. Pray
that she is not allowed any contact with children after her release.

The Winters case is one that many experts find baffling. Although
many serial killers start out as arsonists, most leave their firestarting
ways behind them once they graduate to murder. Winters, however,
was simultaneously a serial killer and a serial arsonist. Her motive for
murder is also somewhat confounding. During her multi-year arson
spree, Winters was often institutionalized, regularly admitting herself
to psychiatric facilities. The doctors who examined her found that she

was not suffering from any particular psychosis but rather from borderline personality disorder, a condition that is exceedingly difficult to treat. This is particularly true when the sufferer (like Winters) refuses to stay on medication.

Much of Winters's problems stemmed from the heavy burden of survivor guilt she carried over the deaths of her siblings. According to her, she'd always believed that she would die on the anniversary of their deaths and lived through each of these dates in morbid fear of her own demise. She was also prone to self-harm and attempted suicide on at least one occasion.

But while self-harm and suicide attempts are not unusual in such cases, Winters is unique in that she directed much of her anger outward. Her frequent arsons appear to have been a way of recreating the deaths of her siblings, with other victims paying a similar price. Her choice of child victims appeared to feed this same obsession. It was as though she was determined that they would not be allowed to enjoy lives that had been denied to her sisters and brother.

FOOTNOTE: Shirley Winters has never been charged with the Hermon, New York fire that claimed the lives of her friend's three children. She has also never admitted to starting the blaze. Given her history, her proximity to the fire, and the date it was set (just a day before she burned her own children to death), it is not a stretch to believe that she was responsible.

Yvonne Fletcher

It is, in many ways, the perfect poison, a colorless, odorless substance that can easily be stirred into food or into a cup of tea, where it will be consumed without raising suspicion. In fact, thallium became so popular as a murder weapon between the 1920s and 1950s that it was dubbed "the poisoner's poison" or half-jokingly "inheritance powder." But the effects of this deadly toxin are no laughing matter. Victims experience excruciating stomach and leg cramps, numbness in the extremities, nausea, vomiting, and diarrhea. Their hair may also start falling out in clumps. Often, they die screaming in agony.

Fortunately, the widespread use of thallium as a murder weapon would be of short duration. By the 1950s, it had been banned from commercial sale in all countries bar one. The sole exception was Australia and, even there, laws were being enacted to keep the toxin out of the hands of would-be poisoners. By 1952, the general public could no longer purchase thallium or thallium-based products in five of Australia's six states. You could still buy it in New South Wales, though, and the reason for that was obvious. Sydney's inner suburbs were suffering from a rat infestation of biblical proportions. There had even been reports of rodents attacking sleeping children.

Thallium had proved to be a very effective rodenticide, and so the poison continued to be sold as a rat poison in New South Wales, marketed under the brand name Thall-rat. And its availability proved just too much of a temptation for some people. Between March 1952 and May 1953, there were at least ten thallium-related deaths in Sydney, resulting in three murder trials and three charges of attempted murder. Some of those brought before the courts would achieve lasting infamy, most notably Caroline Grills. Arguably Australia's most infamous murderess, Grills was a grandmotherly-type who murdered four family members (and attempted to kill several others) by giving them baked goods tainted with thallium. Aunty Thally, as she was dubbed by the press, did it (apparently) for sport.

But sensational as the Grills case proved to be, it wasn't Australia's first high profile thallium poisoning case. Before Caroline Grills, there were Ruby Norton and Beryl Hague. Before either of them, there was Yvonne Gladys Fletcher.

Yvonne Fletcher was a 30-year-old mother-of-two living an unremarkable life in the Sydney suburb of Newtown. She was married to Bertrand "Bluey" Fletcher, a rat catcher by trade and Yvonne's second husband. The marriage, however, was not a happy one. Bluey Fletcher was a violent man who often used his fists on his wife, especially when he'd been drinking. Several times, Yvonne landed up in the hospital and, on one occasion, she needed a blood transfusion after Bluey smashed her nose, resulting in severe blood loss. In an era when the police did not get involved in spousal abuse cases, Yvonne had very little recourse to the law. She did, however, have another outlet.

Given Bluey's occupation, it should be no surprise that there were copious amounts of Thall-rat stored in the Fletcher household. Yvonne started dipping into her husband's stock and stirring small quantities of the toxin into his meals and drinks. Before long, Bluey was showing the classic signs of thallium poisoning. He was afflicted by stomach and leg cramps; he could barely eat anything without throwing up or rushing for the bathroom; his hair was falling out by the handful. Within two weeks of first displaying these debilitating symptoms, Fletcher was dead and his wife was tearfully telling friends and neighbors that he'd likely been killed by his constant workplace exposure to thallium.

And that seemed the most likely explanation. Indeed, Yvonne might well have gotten away with murder had someone not informed the authorities that her first husband, the father of her two children, had died in remarkably similar circumstances. Desmond Butler had passed away on July 29, 1948, after a short illness characterized by the now familiar symptoms. Since he'd worked as a cleaner at Grace Brothers department store, the accidental exposure theory would have been unlikely in his case.

But why might Desmond Butler have been murdered? Looking into the conditions of the Butler marriage provided the police with a possible answer. It had not been a happy union. Like Bluey Fletcher, Butler had been abusive to his wife. He'd also been work shy and a petty criminal. While married to Yvonne, he'd spent two years behind bars, leaving her to care for their two infant daughters. Despite this hardship, Yvonne had survived and had even been able to save a small amount of money. That lasted only until Butler was released. Then he relieved his wife of her hard-earned savings and soon blew it on booze. That perhaps was when Yvonne decided to kill him.

On April 21, 1952, the coroner ordered the exhumation of Desmond Butler's corpse. This order was executed at Rookwood Cemetery the following day under ominously heavy skies. Thereafter, the body was moved to the City Morgue where it was autopsied by Drs. Percy and Sheldon. Samples of tissue were then forwarded to the Government Analyst, Dr. Taylor, for examination. That returned the expected result. Desmond Butler's corpse was found to contain three grams of thallium, suggesting that he'd been fed small amounts of the poison over a protracted period. The only person who could have administered the poison was his wife.

Yvonne Fletcher was arrested on May 19, 1952. She appeared before a packed session of the Central Criminal Court in September 1952, charged with murder. Fletcher's defense denied this, but the forensic evidence was against her. She was found guilty, showing no emotion as the jury foreman read the verdict. However, her response was markedly different when the judge pronounced sentence of death. Then she collapsed in the dock, dropping the prayer book that she'd carried throughout the seven-day trial. She was escorted from the courtroom crying pitifully.

Yvonne Fletcher was taken to Long Bay Prison, where she was placed in an observation cell and put on suicide watch. However, Fletcher would not die in prison, either by her own hand or at the end of the hangman's noose. Her sentence was commuted on appeal to life imprisonment. In her case, life would mean just 12 years. She was paroled from Long Bay in 1964. By then, her case had long been eclipsed in the headlines by that of thallium serial killer, Caroline Grills. Details of Fletcher's life and whereabouts after her release are unknown.

Michele Kalina

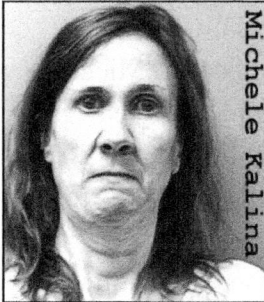

When Michele Kalina moved her family from their house in Berks County to a high-rise apartment in downtown Reading, Pennsylvania, she had only one stipulation. There was a certain closet that they were not to open. Not ever. That was in 2008, and the rule was upheld for two years until October 26, 2010, when curiosity got the better of Kalina's 19-year-old daughter, Elizabeth. She peered into the secret closet and made a discovery that would turn her world on its head and send shock waves through the entire community. Inside were the skeletal remains of five tiny corpses.

To say that Elizabeth was shocked by what she found would be to vastly understate her reaction. She was horrified, sickened, perplexed. How had the dead babies gotten there? She knew the answer to that question, of course. Her mother had put them there. Why else would she have told them to stay away from the closet? But who were they? Where had they come from? Who had killed them? Surely it could not have been her mother. Surely. Distraught and confused, Elizabeth decided to show her father what she'd uncovered.

Jeff Kalina had married Elizabeth's mother back in 1986, after they met at college. Michele was just 19 at the time, and the couple would go on to have two children – Elizabeth, and a son named Andrew, who was born with cerebral palsy and died in 2000 at age 13. By then, Jeff had been struck down by a debilitating disease of his own. He was disabled, wheelchair-bound and entirely reliant on his wife. Michele, to her credit, took on the responsibility without complaint. She began working as a home-help aide for the elderly, putting in as many as 70 hours a week to support her family. And yet she still found time to provide loving care to Jeff and to be an attentive parent to her daughter. Elizabeth would later relate how her mother would often take her to carnivals, amusement parks and other "fun events." Those who knew Michele thought that she was a saint.

But unbeknownst to these admirers, Michele Kalina was living a secret life. In 1996, while working at a home health agency, she had started an affair with a co-worker, a relationship that would endure for fourteen years. During that time, Michele fell pregnant six times, astonishingly managing to keep the pregnancies a secret from her husband and daughter, even from her lover. To him, she spun a fanciful story which was nonetheless believed. She said that she suffered from cysts in her Fallopian tubes which caused her belly to swell up. Later she'd explain the flattening of her midriff by claiming that she had undergone a procedure to drain the cysts. This happened several times during the relationship, and the story was believed each time. In the meanwhile, Michele had secretly given birth to six babies.

But what had happened to the infants? That horrific truth would only come to light after Michele Kalina was arrested and charged with murder. For now, her husband and daughter were faced with a horrible dilemma. Should they cover up the crimes or call the police? Thankfully, they decided to do the right thing.

On October 26, 2010, officers arrived at the Kalina apartment in response to a bizarre 911 call. They were almost certain that it was a hoax, but they were disavowed of that notion when Elizabeth led them to the closet and showed them what was inside. One of the tiny corpses had been placed in a plastic bucket and then encased in concrete; another was contained in a cardboard box; three more had simply been tossed into garbage bags. The police also learned of a sixth child when they discovered a letter written by Michele to her lover in August 2003. In it, she said that she'd given birth to a healthy baby at St. Joseph Medical Center in Reading and had given the little girl up for adoption. That assertion turned out to be true. But what had happened to the other children? How had they died?

Given the advanced state of decomposition, that was going to be difficult to determine. Taken into custody, Michele Kalina initially claimed that all of the infants had been stillborn. She said that she was an alcoholic and had delivered the babies while intoxicated. She also said that she had blacked out and could not remember much about the births. Since five successive stillborn babies was unlikely, the police didn't believe her. They kept probing until Michele eventually admitted that one of the babies had indeed been alive. However, she'd wrapped it too tightly in a towel and had accidentally suffocated it.

This, too, seemed unlikely, not to mention convenient for the accused killer. Later tests would suggest that all of the children had been alive when delivered. That meant that Kalina must have killed them. It made her a serial killer of newborns, a very rare breed of murderer. The only similar case that springs readily to mind is that of Sabine Hilschenz, a German woman who murdered nine of her newborn babies and buried them in flowerpots.

Nonetheless, the pathologist could not state beyond a reasonable doubt that the babies had not been stillborn. When Michele Kalina appeared before a Berks County jury in July 2011, it was for one count of third-degree murder plus several of failing to report the death of a child and abuse of a corpse. She entered guilty pleas to all of the charges, effectively throwing herself on the mercy of the court. Her attorneys then offered mitigating circumstances, stating that Michele had been sexually and emotionally abused as a child and that she suffered from depression, alcoholism, and mental health issues. Jeff Kalina also took the stand to plead his wife's case. He said that Michele was a good woman and that he still loved her, despite the affair. He said also that he would wait for her, if the court decided to give her a custodial sentence.

Kalina was then asked how his wife could have gone through multiple pregnancies without him noticing. Michele was a petite woman; surely he must have seen something? To this, he explained that he and Michele had not been intimate for the last 18 years of their 25-year marriage. He never saw her naked and, although he did notice that she sometimes appeared to be picking up weight, he did not associate that with her being pregnant. There was only one exception. During Michele's 2003 pregnancy, he'd asked his daughter Elizabeth whether she thought her mother might be "with child." Elizabeth had told him that the idea was ridiculous, and he'd left it at that.

Michele Kalina's case had come before the courts at a problematic time for her. Over the previous decade, there'd been a number of high profile cases involving mothers who'd murdered their child. These included Christina Riggs, Andrea Yates, and Marie Noe, and none of those women had gotten off lightly. Riggs had actually been sentenced to death and had subsequently been executed. U.S. juries appeared to be taking a stand against mothers who murdered their children, and the case of Michele Kalina was no different. Despite her guilty plea and her apparent remorse, Kalina received the maximum term for third-degree murder – 20 to 40 years in prison.

Nina Holbrook

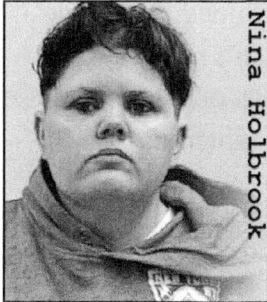

Carl Holbrook had had his troubles with the law over the decades. Back in 1995 and again in 2007, he had been convicted of sexual offences and had done time in prison. In 2011, however, Carl was 50 years old and he was a changed man, living a peaceful life in rural Centerville, Indiana, with only his 30-year-old daughter, Nina, for company. Nina had her own problems, mainly mental health issues for which she was taking medication. Still, the pair seemed happy enough in their cohabitation arrangement. They were quiet and somewhat reclusive. Neighbors barely knew they were there.

But all of that was to change on the afternoon of Friday, July 8, 2011. Carl was expecting a visitor that afternoon. His brother, Harvey, was dropping by. Harv had never visited the house at 10037 Chapel Road before, and although Carl had given him directions, he was afraid that his brother might get lost. It was for this reason that he was standing on the sidewalk, looking down the road in the direction from which he expected Harv to appear. He was still waiting when Nina walked out onto the porch and asked him to come inside. There was something she needed to show him.

Carl was somewhat irritated by the interruption. He told Nina that he was busy right now and would check it out once her Uncle Harv arrived. But Nina was insistent. "It's urgent," she whined. Knowing what his daughter was like, knowing that she wouldn't relent until he did what she wanted, Carl let out a long sigh. He cast one more look down the road and then turned and followed his daughter into the house. Apparently, the "urgent thing" he needed to see was in her bedroom.

The first thing that Carl noticed when he entered the room was a lit candle on the nightstand. "Put that out," he demanded immediately. "What do you want to do? Start a fire?" But Nina wasn't listening. She was reaching for the coffee mug that sat on the stand beside the candle. Now she suddenly turned and flung its contents at him, hitting him square in the face and stinging his eyes. Carl barely had time to register the oily texture of the liquid, the sickeningly sweet kerosene smell. Then Nina thrust the candle in his direction, applying it to his skin. Before Carl could even respond, there was a whoosh and the liquid ignited, engulfing him in a fireball.

Carl let out a scream and started slapping impotently at the flames. "Help me!" he yelled. "For God's sake, Nina. Help me!" Nina, however, was disinclined to help. She was already crossing the room, opening the window and climbing through. As she slid her feet to the ground below, she cast one final look inside and saw her father involved in a deathly dance as he tried in vain to extinguish the flames. Already the sickening aroma of singed hair and seared flesh fouled the air. Nina wasn't waiting around to see more. She calmly rounded the house, walked down the path and through the gate. Then she set off down the road, walking at a leisurely pace.

There would be two more sightings of Nina Holbrook that afternoon. Some way down the road, she encountered her Uncle Harv on his way to visit her father. She offered a jovial greeting. When Harv asked if her father was home, Nina said simply, "I torched him. I set him alight." Harv didn't know what to make of that statement, although he was well aware that his niece was prone to bizarre outbursts. Nonetheless, he quickened his pace.

Some way farther on, Nina was spotted by a neighbor, Kyle Carpenter, who thought that her facial expression looked odd. "Are you all right?" Carpenter asked.

"No, sir, I'm fine," Nina responded. "Thank you very much for asking." She then gave him a thumbs up and continued on her way.

By now, Harvey Holbrook had reached the house and come upon a horrific scene. His brother was lying on the floor, all of the clothes burned from his body, the skin underneath blackened. Harv immediately called 911, bringing police and paramedics racing to the scene. It was decided right away that Carl would have to be taken to the specialist burns unit at Miami Valley Hospital in Dayton, Ohio. A helicopter was called in to make the transfer, but despite the best efforts of doctors, Carl did not survive. His injuries were just too severe. He had literally been burned alive.

Catching the perpetrator was not a problem for the police. Nina Holbrook was found wandering aimlessly around the neighborhood later that afternoon. But getting to the motive of this horrific crime was less straightforward. Nina was happy to discuss how she had committed the murder – she'd flung a cupful of lighter fluid into her father's face and then applied a flame to it – but she was unwilling (or unable) to say why she had done it. That left investigators to speculate. Had Carl, a convicted sex offender, been up to his old tricks? Had he been molesting his daughter? Had this been her revenge? Or was the explanation simpler than that. Had Nina forgotten to take her meds and suffered a mental breakdown? No one could say for certain.

But the lack of motive would not be an impediment to prosecuting this case, not when the perpetrator willingly admitted her guilt. The question was whether she was mentally competent to stand trial. Her lawyer, Stephen Rabe, had already indicated that he intended raising an insanity defense if the matter ever came before a judge.

In the end, a compromise was reached between defense and prosecution. Holbrook would plead guilty but mentally ill to charges of felony murder and arson. In exchange, the state agreed to set her sentence at 55 years for murder and 50 years for arson, to run concurrently. The first part of that sentence would be served at Logansport State Hospital, with periodic evaluations to determine if and when she was well enough to enter the general prison system. With those terms agreed, Holbrook accepted her punishment, less 1,453 days credit for time served while awaiting trial.

Nina Holbrook is current being held at the Fort Wayne County Jail. She has never revealed why she subjected her father to such a horrific and agonizing death.

Kristin Rossum

The scene looked like something out of the movie, American Beauty. On the bed lay the body of 26-year-old Greg de Villers, unresponsive despite the best efforts of paramedics. Nearby stood his wife of less than two years, Kristin Rossum. It was she who'd found the body, she who'd called 911. The American Beauty touch came from the red rose petals scattered across the bed covers. Greg must have placed them there himself, Kristin insisted, just before he'd taken his own life. It was a message to her. American Beauty was, after all, her favorite movie.

Kristen was equally frank when police questioned her regarding the possible reason for her husband's suicide. They'd been having marital problems, she said, and she'd recently asked for a trial separation. According to her, Greg had become increasingly "clingy" since their June 1999 wedding. She'd felt suffocated by his attention and had told him that she needed her space. He'd taken it badly, sinking into an ever-deepening depression. He'd also begun drinking heavily. Now, it appeared, he'd taken his own life.

Or had he? Greg's family conceded that he'd been drinking too much
of late but insisted that he would never have killed himself. And he
most definitely would not have injected himself with some drug, as
was suspected. He hated needles. The family believed that he had been
murdered. And if that were the case, then there could only be one
suspect.

The San Diego police were now left with a conundrum to solve. Was it
murder or was it suicide? Could the beautiful and accomplished
Kristen Rossum really have killed her husband? What possible motive
could she have had?

On the face of it, Kristin made a very unlikely killer. The daughter of
two college professors, she'd gone on to graduate summa cum laude
from San Diego State University with a degree in chemistry.
Thereafter, she'd found employment as a toxicologist at the Medical
Examiner's office, where her work performance was rated as excellent
by her superiors. Away from the office, she and Greg appeared to have
a solid, loving relationship. They'd been together for nearly seven
years, dating for five years before tying the knot.

That was the picture as an outsider might perceive it. But as detectives
started delving a little deeper into Kristen's background, they learned
that it was not quite the fairy tale that it appeared to be. The former
child model had a dark side. Back in high school, she'd been a
straight-A student until the age of 16, when she had discovered crystal
meth. Then her grades had plummeted and she'd begun to neglect her
personal appearance and was losing weight. She had also begun
stealing from her parents and had become a habitual liar. On one
occasion, she'd slashed her wrists during an argument with her father,

an alarming development that had prompted her parents to enroll her in a drug rehab program. It was the first of many interventions that Ralph and Constance Rossum would attempt. None of them worked. Kristen would stay clean for a while and then start using again.

In 1994, Ralph and Constance used their collective influence to withdraw Kristen from Claremont High School and enroll her part time at the University of Redlands in suburban Los Angeles. For a while, that move seemed to have the desired effect, but then the Rossums made the crucial mistake of allowing their daughter to move into a dorm on campus. Before long, she was using again, and by Christmas, she'd dropped out and disappeared across the border into Mexico. It was there, in the raucous party town of Tijuana, that she met Greg de Villers.

For Greg, the handsome son of a prominent plastic surgeon, it was love at first sight. Within weeks, he and Kristen were an item and Greg had committed himself to helping her kick her drug habit. That would be a rocky road but Greg was in it for the long haul. He encouraged Kristen to resume her studies, and (again with the help of her parents) she enrolled at San Diego State University. There she excelled, with one professor describing her as one of the most promising students he'd ever tutored. Eventually, she'd graduate summa cum laude. Soon after, Greg proposed and Kristen said yes. They married in June 1999.

Greg and Kristen appeared to all who knew them as if they were a storybook couple. They were both attractive and intelligent, both had good jobs. They were affectionate to one another in public and appeared hopelessly in love. But, for Kristen at least, much of that was a front. She had never been fully committed to the marriage and had spoken to her mother about calling it off before the wedding. Constance had convinced her that it was just a case of prenuptial nerves and had convinced her to go ahead with it. But within weeks of the nuptials, Kristen was telling a friend that she felt like a bird trapped in a cage. "I married the wrong person," she confided.

If Greg de Villers was aware of his wife's unhappiness, he said nothing about it to anyone else. To him, everything appeared to be going swimmingly. He was building a career for himself at a biotech company while Kristin was working at the San Diego Medical Examiner's Office. He was telling friends that he planned on spending the rest of his life with Kristen and hoped to start a family with her. Unbeknownst to him, the woman he'd devoted his life to had already violated their marital vows.

Kristen's lover was a man named Michael Robertson, an Australian national who happened to be her supervisor at the M.E.'s office. Like Kristen, Robertson was married, but that did not stop him flirting with her literally from her first day on the job. Neither did it prevent her from responding in kind. In no time at all, they were involved in a torrid affair, and Kristen was telling a friend that she had met the love of her life.

It is not clear exactly how Greg found out about his wife's infidelity. According to Kristen, it was she who told him, and it was that revelation that had led, inadvertently, to him taking his own life. He'd taken the news hard and had begun drinking heavily, all the while sinking into an ever-deepening depression. At one point, he'd called Michael Robertson at work and demanded that he stop seeing his wife. Robertson had said that the decision was Kristen's to make, and the relationship continued. It all culminated on the night of November 6, when Kirsten called 911 and reported that her husband was unresponsive.

This, at least, was the story that Kristen Rossum told the police. But there was one important detail that she had omitted. At the time of her affair with Robertson, she had relapsed and was using drugs again – methamphetamine as well as various prescription medications. Might that have formed part of her motive for killing Greg de Villers? Over time, the police would suspect that it had. They developed a theory that Greg had made a desperate play to end his wife's affair. He told Kristen that unless she broke off with Robertson, he'd call her bosses and tell them that she was using drugs. He would also expose her relationship with Robertson and they'd both be fired. Faced with the prospect of losing both her job and her lover, Kristen had then decided to kill her husband.

A postmortem would, of course, provide a clearer picture, but investigators had a problem. Their suspect worked at the medical examiner's office, causing a potential conflict of interest. The situation was resolved when the police outsourced the autopsy to a private lab in Los Angeles. Soon they'd deliver a bombshell. Greg de Villers had died from an overdose of a painkiller called fentanyl, a drug so rarely prescribed that the Los Angeles lab was one of the few facilities in the country that was able to test for it. The levels in de Villers's blood were seven times the lethal dosage.

And that raised a number of questions. If Greg had indeed committed suicide, how had he obtained the drug? How had he administered it? Why were no traces of it found at his residence?

Addressing those questions one by one, the police uncovered some interesting clues. Firstly, there was no indication that fentanyl had ever been prescribed to Greg. The drug was, however, kept at the Medical Examiner's offices, and a vial of it was missing from stock. Investigators also learned that, because of its rarity, the San Diego M.E. never ran checks for fentanyl while running an autopsy. Kristen would have known that and might have used it for that very reason.

As to how the drug had been administered, it was learned that it could be taken orally or injected. In this case, the body had an unexplained puncture mark, suggesting the latter. Given Greg's aversion for needles, it seemed unlikely that he'd have injected himself. Even if he had, where was the syringe? Where was the rest of the vial? The only conclusion was that someone had removed it from the scene, and that person could only have been Kristen Rossum. The theory developed by investigators was that she'd waited for Greg to fall asleep and had then injected him with a lethal dose of the painkiller.

On June 25, 2001, seven months after her husband's death, Rossum was arrested and charged with murder. She was later released on $1.25 million bond, put up by her parents. At the subsequent trial, the prosecution contended that Kristin had killed her husband in order to keep him from revealing her affair and drug use. The defense, meanwhile, was sticking to the story that Kristen had told from the start – that Greg de Villers had been deeply distressed over her affair and had killed himself as a result. Rossum's attorney even suggested that Greg had concealed the evidence after giving himself the fatal injection. This, he said, was a final attempt by Greg to get back at his cheating wife.

It was an implausible story and one that the jury was disinclined to accept. In November 2002, it returned a verdict of guilty to the charge of first-degree murder. A month later, on December 12, Kristen Rossum was sentenced to life in prison without the possibility for parole. She is currently held at the Central California Women's Facility in Chowchilla and still maintains that she is guilty of nothing but adultery. As for Michael Robertson, he was fired from his job once the details of the affair became public. He has since fled back to Australia and has never been charged with any offense related to the murder.

For more True Crime books by Robert Keller please visit

       http://bit.ly/kellerbooks

Printed in Dunstable, United Kingdom

66927883R00078